LETTERS TO MY MOTHER

LETTERS TO MY MOTHER

A Message of Love, A Plea for Freedom

INGRID BETANCOURT

Mélanie Delloye-Betancourt

Lorenzo Delloye-Betancourt

Foreword by Elie Wiesel

Introduction by Dominique Simonnet

ABRAMS IMAGE • NEW YORK

CONTENTS

FOREWORD

Read this letter. Read it carefully. The voice that speaks to you on these pages will keep you awake at night.

The life she endures in the jungle, day after endless day among the disciples of violence and hatred–she sets it down in language both simple and heartrending. She tells of her loneliness, her homesickness, her anguish approaching despair. Imprisoned, tormented, tortured, abandoned by too many for too long, buried in the distant shadows of terror–we might believe her silenced, or dead.

Her captors have tried to deprive her of her gifts–her intelligence, her sensitivity. They have tried to isolate her even more by driving her mad.

But Ingrid Betancourt remains lucid. And courageous, even heroic. And free.

This fighter for mankind's freedom tells us that for her "It is better not to want anything so as to be free, at least, of desires." But in fact she does have desires–simple desires, and deeply moving: to hold up her head in defiance of torturers and butchers; to retain, despite everything, faced with the brutality of evil, her dignity and her faith in man.

In the name of her humanity, and of yours, I implore you to listen to this voice.

For you, it is such a small thing. For her, it is a message from the heart, a moving gesture of solidarity.

ELIE WIESEL

INTRODUCTION

"I dedicate these lines to those who are my oxygen, my life— to those who keep my head above water, who do not let me drown into oblivion, emptiness, and despair. . . . What they have done for us has made all the difference: they have made us feel human."

Ingrid Betancourt

The words that you are about to read come from hell, from a forsaken corner of our planet where laws, virtues, the rights of man—even the simple word human—no longer have any meaning, where women and men, snatched from their families, are now prisoners, shackled, treated like animals year after year. This book is a cry in the wilderness, a message in a bottle cast into the sea by Ingrid Betancourt, who was taken hostage in the Colombian jungle on February 23, 2002. It is even more than that; it is a declaration of love, a strike for freedom, a lesson in humanity.

Have you heard the story? Perhaps you'd rather not. . . . Some 2,200 miles from the United States, in a country so luxuriant and fertile that it might be mistaken for a second Eden, 17,000 fanatical guerrillas, claiming to follow an archaic Marxist ideology, make a living from trafficking drugs and human beings. Calling themselves the Revolutionary Armed Forces of Colombia, or FARC (Fuerzas Armadas Revolucionarias de Colombia), this organization has fought the Colombian government for nearly forty years in a civil war that has ripped the country apart, subjecting its citizens to daily violence, kidnappings, and illegal detentions. FARC uses hostages like currency for its sordid financial transactions. It also holds "political" hostages–members of congress, military men, civil servants–as shields against military intervention. Among these victims is Ingrid Betancourt, as well as three American citizens who were taken hostage on February 13, 2003.

In many countries around the world, Ingrid Betancourt has become a symbol of liberty and the fight against barbarity. Born in 1961 to a diplomat father (minister of education in Colombia, and later UNESCO ambassador to Colombia in Paris) and a mother who championed the cause of the street children of Bogotá, Ingrid Betancourt divided her time between France, where she studied, the United States, and Colombia. Disgusted with the political situation in Colombia, she became engaged in politics, leading an incessant and courageous fight against corruption and drug traffickers. The young woman immediately created a wave of hope when she was first elected to Colombia's Chamber of Representatives, where she tirelessly denounced the links between certain politicians and drug trafficking; four years later she was triumphantly elected senator.

In 2002, while running for president as head of the independent party that she had created, Ingrid Betancourt was seized by FARC on a Colombian road. Not until the summer of 2003 did her family receive a brief video message, explaining that she had been taken hostage. Long months of silence followed.

Over the years the movement for her release has grown, not only in France but also all over Europe. Though there was no definite evidence that she was even still alive, she was named an honorary citizen of many French cities. In Paris, huge portraits of her were hung on the Hotel de Ville and on the gates of the Luxembourg Gardens. Diplomatic action intensified; her cause was mentioned in many international meetings. In 2007, just after his election as president of France, Nicolas Sarkozy declared the release of Ingrid Betancourt an absolute priority of his government. Emissaries were sent from France to a number of countries, notably to Latin America, to urge the Colombian government and FARC to accept a "humanitarian accord" and exchange hostages–among them Ingrid Betancourt–for imprisoned guerrillas. Responding to this pressure, Venezuelan president Hugo Chávez offered his services in an attempt at mediation.

On December 1, 2007, during the arrest of some guerrillas in Bogotá, the Colombian police confiscated a video that included messages from the three American hostages to their families, as well as a short clip of Ingrid Betancourt, alive, emaciated, and drained, but still defiant toward her tormentors. The video was accompanied by a long letter, dated October 24, 2007, 8:34 A.M., written by Ingrid to her mother and her family, "on a morning overcast, like my spirit." In twelve pages filled with a regular, cramped hand, with no space left blank and no words altered, Ingrid, "weary of suffering" and tempted to yield to despair, tries to put the essential into words.

That deeply moving letter, published here in its entirety, is an impassioned declaration of love to her family, her children, and all those dear to her, and at the same time a magnificent defense of liberty. From the depths of the jungle, she appeals to humanity, sharing her deep feelings for France, which championed her cause, and praising the United States and the great spirit of the Founding Fathers that created that nation. "When Lincoln defended the right to life and the freedom of the black slaves of America. . . Many economic and political interests were considered more important than the life and liberty of a handful of blacks. But Lincoln was victorious, and today the priority of human life over economic and political interests has become part of the culture of that nation."

This is Ingrid Betancourt. With a rare and lucid intelligence, this imprisoned woman at the edge of the abyss speaks of love and liberty. Unquestionably, her letter will stand as one of the great texts of history. It is this universal resonance that Nobel Peace Prize Laureate Elie Wiesel, personally engaged in the fight for Betancourt's release, evokes in the foreword to this book. For his generosity we are infinitely thankful.

Ingrid Betancourt's message could not go unanswered. From her home in New York, her twenty-two-year-old daughter Mélanie, who has rallied public opinion and governments to save her mother since she was sixteen, along with her brother Lorenzo, also put pen to paper. The two children, who sent messages to their mother over Colombian radio night after night, hoping that she might hear them, have written a dignified and poignant letter to her in an attempt to counter her captors' barbarity, and to offer their mother a lifeline: "Let our words, which come to you drip by drip over the radio, be your energy. Let our thoughts, which we send to you in secret, be your comfort. We will not forsake you, Mama."

On January 10, 2008, two Colombian women—Clara Rojas, Ingrid Betancourt's campaign manager, who was captured with her in 2002, and former congresswoman Consuelo González—were released by FARC to Venezuelan president Hugo Chávez, an event that has revived hope for Ingrid

Betancourt and the other hostages. The simultaneous publication of this book in a number of countries is an act of urgency. It hopes to rally the conscience of the entire world to obtain as soon as possible, through humanitarian accords and through all the diplomatic negotiation possible, the freedom of Ingrid Betancourt and the other hostages who have been imprisoned in the jungle for the past ten years. The two "Letters to My Mother" printed here, writings evoking a hell on earth that exists here and now, writings straight from the heart, not only tell the terrible drama of these Colombian hostages but also encompass all the suffering and all the grandeur that is mankind.

DOMINIQUE SIMONNET

INGRID BETANCOURT'S LETTER

Colombian Jungle
Wednesday, October 24
8:34 A.M.

Morning overcast, like my spirit

My beloved and divine Mamita of my heart,

Every day I wake up thanking God that I have you. Every day I open my eyes at 4 A.M. and get ready to be wide awake to listen to your message on the *Carrilera de las 5* program. My daily joy consists of hearing your voice, sensing your love, your tenderness, your steadfastness, and your devotion to the commitment of never leaving my side. Every day I pray to God to bless you, to care for you, protect you, and allow me the opportunity to one day indulge you in everything, to please you in everything, to have you like a queen close to me; since I cannot bear the thought of being separated from you again. This is very dense jungle where the sunlight scarcely ever penetrates, and it is barren of affection, sympathy, or tenderness. That is why your voice is my umbilical cord to life. I dream of hugging you so tight that I become imbedded in you. I dream of saying to you, "Never again, Mamita, will you weep for me in this life or the next." I have kept praying to God to allow me to prove to you how much you mean to me, to take care of you, and not to abandon you for a single moment. In planning my life, should I be set free one day, Mamita darling, consider living with us–or with me. No more messages, no more telephone calls, no more separations; I don't want there to be one single meter between you and me. Because I know that everybody can live without me, except you. I sustain myself each day with that dream of the two of us, in due time we will see how God will provide the way and we will organize ourselves. But the first thing I want to say to you is that without you, I would not have been able to endure till now.

Each day you ask me how I am doing. I know that Pinchao[1] has given you many details, and I bless and thank him for having told you everything. I admire Pinchao enormously. What he did was heroic. One day, God willing, I will give him a tremendous hug, like the one I couldn't give him when he left the camp. Help him in every way possible, particularly if he has to seek asylum. Tell him how much I love him and of the thanks I have given God that he came out alive from his exploit. Well, things got harsher for us after Pinchao escaped. Extreme measures were taken that have made it terrible for me. They separated me from the people with whom I had a good rapport and affection and put me in with a very difficult group. I am tired, Mamita, tired of suffering. I have been, or tried to be, strong. These nearly six years of captivity have proven that I am not as resistant, not as brave, not as intelligent, not as strong as I thought. I have put up many battles, have tried to escape several times, have tried to keep up hope like one keeps one's head above water. But, Mamita darling, I give up. I would like to think that one day I will get out of here, but I

---

1. John Frank Pinchao, a Colombian policeman, was a FARC hostage for almost nine years. He successfully escaped in May 2007 after having marched seventeen days in the jungle. He recounts having spent almost three years in captivity with Ingrid Betancourt.

realize that what happened to the congressmen[2]–which affect-
ed me so deeply–could happen to me at any moment. I believe
it would be a relief for everybody. I feel that my children are
on "standby" with their lives waiting for me to get out. Your
daily suffering, and everybody else's, makes death appear
to me almost a sweet option. To be with my dear Papito[3], for
whom I have mourned every day for the past four years. I keep
thinking that at last I am going to cry no more, that it has now
healed over. But the pain starts up again and attacks me like a
vicious dog, and I again feel my heart breaking into pieces. I
am tired of suffering, of bearing it all inside me all the time, of
lying to myself, of believing that this will soon end and finding
that every new day is the same hell as the one before. I think of
my children, my three children, of Sebastián[4], Mela, and Loli[5].
We have gone through so much together, have lived our lives
so intensely that terra firma seems to have disappeared in the
distance. They are the same, and yet they have changed, and
with every second of absence, of my inability to be there for
them, to assuage their pain, to be able to advise them or give
them strength and patience and humility in the face of life's
blows, all the lost opportunities to be their *mamá*, poison
these moments of infinite loneliness for me, as if I were given
an intravenous injection of cyanide. Mamita darling, this is a
very difficult moment for me. They demand a proof of life and

2. In June 2007, FARC announced the execution of eleven provincial deputies,
shot in the head at close range, who had been taken hostage in 2002. Their
families had attempted mediation several times, and some were very close to
being successful.
3. Gabriel Betancourt, Ingrid's father, who was minister of education and Colombian ambassador to UNESCO, was very close to his daughter. He died a month
to the day after her abduction.
4. Sebastián, Ingrid's stepson and Fabrice Delloye's son from a previous marriage.
5. Mélanie and Lorenzo Delloye-Betancourt, Ingrid's children.

here I am pouring my heart out to you on this sheet of paper. I am in poor physical condition. I haven't being eating; my appetite has shut down; my hair is falling out in clumps; I have no desire for anything. And I think the latter is the only thing that is right–having no desire for anything. Because here in this jungle the only answer to everything is "No." It is better not to want anything so as to be free, at least, of desires. I have been asking for an encyclopedic dictionary for the last three years in order to have something to read, to learn something, to keep intellectual curiosity alive. I keep waiting for them to get me one out of compassion but it is better not to think about it. Thereafter, anything at all is a miracle, even hearing you in the mornings, because the radio I have is very old and damaged. Always try to come on, as you do, at the beginning of the broadcast because lately it is picking up a lot of interference and after 5:20 I can only guess at what is being said. Also, when there is important news (Astrid's wedding, for instance), repeat it in several messages. I didn't find out about Astrid and Daniel until last Christmas. Surely, you had mentioned it but I didn't hear that message.

I would now like to go back to the subject of the radio. I would like to ask you, Mamita darling, to tell the children that I want them to send me three messages a week, on Mondays, Wednesdays, and Fridays. Ask them to send you a couple of lines to your e-mail address so that you can read them to me. Nothing world-shaking, just whatever they can think of to write, such as "Mamita, today is a marvelous day" or "I'm having lunch with María; I love her very much and I know you are going to be pleased with her" or "I'm exhausted but I learned a lot today in class about new filming techniques that I'm excited about." I don't need anything more, but I do need to be in contact with them. In fact, every day I wait anxiously to see if you are going to mention them or if you talked with them. That is what makes me happy, the only thing I care about knowing, the only vital, significant, indispensable information. All the rest doesn't matter to me. I want Sebas to write to me, too. I want to know what he is doing: work, love life, etc., etc. Oh! I am 100 percent in agreement with you not calling me at daybreak on Sunday[6]. It pains me greatly to think of you staying up nights and the hours of waiting, and the strain and all. I continue listening to the program out of solidarity with the others but knowing that you are warm asleep in your little bed is restful for me.

Well, as I was telling you, life here is no life; it is a gruesome waste of time. I live, or survive, in a hammock strung between two poles, covered with mosquito netting and a canvas that acts as a roof, which makes me feel like I have a house. I have a shelf on which to keep my belongings, that is to say, the knapsack with my clothes and a bible, my only luxury. Everything is prepared for leaving on the run. Here, nothing is one's own, nothing lasts; uncertainty and precariousness are the only constant. The order is given at any moment to pack up and one gets to sleep stretched out anywhere like an animal. Those are the particularly difficult moments for me. My palms sweat, my mind gets foggy, and I end up doing things twice as slowly as normal. The marches are a calvary because my baggage is very heavy and I can't handle it. Sometimes, the guerrillas carry things of mine to lighten my load, leaving "the pots" for me, which is to say the toiletries which are the

---

6. Every Sunday, the weekly radio broadcast *Las Voces del Secuestro (Voices of the Kidnapped)* transmits the words of the families of hostages, sending messages of hope to those waiting in the jungle.

heaviest, but all of it is a strain. Things of mine are lost or taken, like the jeans that Mela had given me for Christmas, which I was wearing when I was kidnapped. I never saw them again. All I could save was the jacket, which was a blessing because the nights are freezing and I had nothing else for protection. Before, I enjoyed each bath in the river. Being the only woman in the group I have to be practically covered up: shorts, blouse, and boots. So, I bathe like our grandmothers did. Before, I used to enjoy swimming in the river. Now, I don't even look forward to that. I'm weak, chilly, like a cat approaching the water. I, who used to love the water, can hardly recognize myself. During the day I was accustomed to doing two or nearly three hours of exercises. I had invented a contraption, like a small bench made of sticks of wood that I baptized "the step" for doing calisthenics. The idea is to walk up and down on it like on stairs. It has the advantage of not requiring much space, since sometimes the camps they set up are so small that one is practically on top of another prisoner. However, since they separated the groups, I haven't had either the interest or energy for anything. I do some stretching because stress tightens my neck and it is very painful. With stretches, splits, and other exercises I manage to relax the neck tension. That's all, Mamita. I try to keep quiet, to talk as little as possible to avoid trouble. A woman's presence among all those prisoners who have been in captivity for eight to ten years is a problem. I listen to the RFI and BBC on the shortwave radio; I write little because the notebooks pile up and carrying them is torture. I have already burned four. Besides, on the searches, they take away whatever one is most anxious to keep. A letter from you written after the last proof of life in 2003, the sketches by Anastasia and Stanis[7],

7. Anastasia and Stanis, Ingrid's niece and nephew.

the photos of Mela and Loli, my Papá's scapular, notes on a government program of 190 points that I had been writing all these years were taken away. Every day less and less of myself remains. Pinchao already mentioned the rest of the details to you. Everything is hard. That's the reality.

It is important that I dedicate these lines to those who are my oxygen, my life–to those who keep my head above water, who do not let me drown into oblivion, emptiness, and despair. They are you, my children, Astrica[8] and her little ones, Fab[9], Aunt Nancy, and Juanqui[10].

First, give my blessing to my children, the three of them, Sebastián, Mela, and Loli, so that it may accompany them on every step they take. I am in communication with God, Jesus, and the Virgin every day. I commend them to God so that their faith shall never falter, and so that they never separate from Him. Tell them that they have never ceased to be my source of joy in this harsh captivity. Everything here has two sides, joy comes with pain, happiness is sad, love cures and opens new wounds; to remember is to live and to die anew. For years, I was unable to think of the children, and the pain of my Papá's death overflowed all my capacity to bear up. When I thought of them I would feel as though I was smothering, that I couldn't breathe. Then I would say to myself "Fab is there; he takes care of everything, no need to think, no need to think." I nearly went mad on the death of my father. I must talk to Astrica to do my mourning. I never knew how it happened, who was with him, if he left me a message, a letter, a blessing. But, with the years, what has alleviated my torment is the thought that he died trusting in God and that one day I will be there to hug

8. Astrid, Ingrid's sister.

9. Fabrice Delloye, Ingrid's ex-husband and the father of her children.

10. Juan-Carlos, Ingrid's husband.

him. Of that I am certain. Feeling that you are strong has been my strength. I did not hear messages until I joined "Lucho" Eladio Pérez[11] on August 22, 2003, on his daughter Carope's birthday. We were bosom friends; they separated us in August. However, during all that time he was my support, my escort, my brother. Tell Ángela, Sergio, Laura, Marianita, and Carope that I carry them in my heart as though they were my family. Since that time I have heard your messages with the most unbelievable consistency—you have never failed me. God bless you. I was telling you that for years I was unable to think of the children because of the dreadful pain it caused me not being with them. Now I can hear them and feel more joy than pain. I seek them in my remembrances and sustain myself with the images I keep in my memory of the ages of each. I sing "Happy Birthday" to them on every birthday. I requested permission to make a cake. They used to indulge me and I would do something to celebrate the date. But, for the last three years, every time I ask, the answer is "No." Likewise, if they bring a cookie or some dish of rice and beans, which is the usual thing, I make believe it is a cake and I celebrate their birthdays in my heart. I want you to know that April 8, September 6, and October 1 are sacred to me. I also celebrate December 31, July 18, August 9, September 1, June 24, and October 31. (The last two are for Nancy and Pachao, if I am not mistaken.)

To my Mela, my springtime sunshine, my princess of the swan constellation, whom I so adore, I would like to tell her that I am the proudest mother on earth. I have been so lucky, so blessed by God, to have these children of mine, and this Mela of mine is like life's grand prize. Since she was five years old and able to argue with me intelligently and politely, I have

11. A senator taken by FARC in June 2001.

had, and have, the utmost admiration for my Mela. She possesses more than enough wisdom and enlightenment. And, if I were to die today, I would go satisfied with life, thanking God for my children. I am happy about her master's degree in New York. That is precisely what I would have advised her to do. Her passion is film and I am 100 percent with her in everything. However, take note: it is important for her to do her DOCTORATE. In today's world, you must have credentials even to breathe. To access a doctorate is to be in another sphere, another world, of higher demand and discipline. And it means getting acquainted with the best of the best. I will not flag in insisting with Loli and Mela that they do not falter in getting their Ph.Ds. I would like Mela to promise me that she will do it, that she is going to search the Internet from now on even though it may seem to her still remote and distant, that she is going to become familiar with the curriculums of Harvard, Stanford, and Yale, etc. And that she is going to check out the doctorates offered, in whatever most intrigues her—history, philosophy, archaeology, theology—that she seeks and dreams and becomes enthusiastic, and makes it her personal mission. I know that she wants to work; we are all driven by the challenge of producing and knowing who we really are, but it is something that must be set down in their plans for life. The greater the effort, the greater the achievement; the greater the opportunities, the broader the universe to which you can accede. My Mela, you know that this is vital. It fascinated me that you studied philosophy and not political science; it fascinated me that you undertook learning Italian and Russian. If I have the opportunity, if life grants it to me, I will try to catch up with you! I am your number-one fan. I don't have the words to tell you how highly I assess your career plans, the clear-sightedness of your decisions, the maturity of the road you've chosen, and how you are following it. I know that the film school you are attending is a must and for that I tip my hat to you. I have always told you that you are the best, much better than me, something like the best version of what I wanted to be. For that reason, with the experience I have garnered in my life, and with the perspective the world gives, watching you from this distance, I beg you, my dearest, that you prepare yourself for reaching the top.

To my Lorenzo, my Lollipop, my angel of light, my king of the blue waters, my chief musician, who sings to me and delights me. To the owner of my heart, I would like to tell him that from the day he was born until now, he has been my well-spring of pleasure. Everything that comes from him is balm for my spirit, it comforts me, pacifies me, gives me pleasure, and tranquility. He is my wonder child, my tiny scrap of the sun. How I yearn to see him, kiss him, hug him, listen to him! At last, I was able to hear his voice a couple of times this year! It made me tremble with emotion. It's my Loli; it's the voice of my boy, but now there's another male voice over the boyish one, the gruffness of a man, like my Papá's. Could he have inherited my Papá's hands, those huge, beautiful hands I so sorely miss? Could it be that God gave me that double gift? The other day I clipped a photograph from a newspaper that I happened to pick up. It is an ad for a Carolina Herrera perfume 212 Sexy Men, in which a young boy appears and I thought my Lorenzo must look like him, and I put it away. I love you so much, my darling; I recall when you sang on the Planetarium roof; I always knew that you had the soul of an artist and the voice of an angel. I feel blessed by God that you play the guitar like a god! You must remember the woman who came to the house to give you lessons when you were a kid. I can still see you! It always intrigued me that the teacher told me you were a very good student although I never heard you practicing. But I do remember how those bright little eyes would shine with happiness whenever the teacher came for the class and when she left. I recall that so well. And so many other things, my dear one. I have such a yearning to curl up and go to sleep holding you in my arms like we used to do before they seized me. Such a yearning to cover you with little kisses, and to hear you, to talk to you for hours so that you can tell me everything and I can tell you everything. I knew that you got a 13.75 in your bachelor's. I tell you that you beat me. How proud I am of you, my darling. I am delighted with your double diploma in law and economics at the Sorbonne. Excellent. I'm delighted. I think you shouldn't disregard political science. They are the same special courses if you take economy and finances. Think it over, you could take the exam in September 2008, you will already have had a year at the Sorbonne. It is a prestigious school that opens all the doors for you that you wish. And you can do it, you are brilliant. But keep this in mind, don't neglect your music, you have it in your genes. And like with Mela, I insist you get a master's, then a Ph.D. You have your life ahead of you. You must try to reach the top; to study is to grow, not only for what you learn intellectually, but for the human experience. The people around you will feed you emotionally, will teach you to have greater control over yourself, and will help you to spiritually form a character of service for others, where the ego is reduced to its minimal expression and grows in humility and moral strength. One goes with the other. That's living: to grow in order to serve. For that reason, your music is so important. With it you can bring happiness, compassion, solidarity, and commitment. And with your career you can understand how our society, codes, and regulations function and, also, solutions for achieving a better world. I say the same to both of you, I am so thankful of being the *mamá* of human beings who are so special and who dazzle me to such a degree. I am 100 percent with you, my dear one—with you in everything and for you in whatever you wish. Yes, I am your number-one fan, I even cut out pictures of my idol as if I were a teenager. Thank you for giving me so much happiness.

To my beloved Sebastián, my *Babou bleu*, my little prince of astral and ancestral trips. I have so much I want to tell him! First, that I do not want to leave this world without his having the knowledge, assurance, and confirmation that there are not two but three soul children of mine, whom God has given me and who are inscribed as such in the book of life. I keep him close to my heart day after day, remembering him as I first saw him in his Zorro costume when he was five years old and his little blue eyes were discovering a world that was changing too rapidly. It is for hours that I want to talk to him, to my Mela, and to my Loli. That's it, with him I will have to untangle years of silence in this captivity that weigh too heavily upon me. To tell him that my favorite color is the blue of his eyes with a speck of the light purple in a shawl that he gave me years ago at the Seychelles. I am going to dress myself often in that light purple if I get out of the green prison of this jungle. And I want him to teach me to moonwalk, and so many other things I want to learn from him. But, mainly, I want him to know that I consider him very good-looking, like his mother, very intelligent, like his father, and that he has inherited my same character, which may sometimes be an advantage. But, generally, it is a great karma. That is why each time I think of you my darling, I laugh at the two of us, at you and me. How we have gone round and round only to end up exactly where we started: loving each other with all our hearts. Yes, my *Babou*, I must talk to you, I ask your forgiveness for so many moments when I was not up to it, for my immaturity when I had to protect you and enfold you in my love, and give you strength for living. I ask you to forgive me for not having dared to seek you out, to go for you, to tell you: "Everything can change except my love for you." In case I don't get out of here, I write it so you can keep it in your soul, my beloved *Babou*, and so that you understand what I understood when your brother and sister were born, that I have loved you always as the son that you are and whom God gave me. The rest are formalities.

I must talk of my Fab right now. How can I not tell him that those children of ours are my happiness? That the happiest moments of my life are set in the framework of his love and his presence, his wit and vitality, that our children are shining lights. As my Papá said to Astrid and me, "Your children are splendiferous!" And I turn to Fab because it is to him that I owe all this, the life that I have led interwoven with the thread of unconditional love that never parted, with that eternal commitment of love for one another above all else, that we swore to in Monguí and have never failed to fulfill. Love and only love can explain what we are, he and I, not with the conventions and rituals of the world, but with the spirit of God's love that provides all without condition. I know that Fab has suffered much on my account. I hope his suffering has surcease in knowing that he has been the wellspring of my peace. This test that God sent us is for us to grow so that we may be better human beings, so that we can discard all that is of no use and only weighs down the human spirit. We are traveling the road together even though we are separated. And our effort and struggle is light for our children. He is my greatest consolation; because he is there I know that my children are well and if they are well, none of the rest is grave. Tell Fab that I lean upon him, cry on his shoulder. In him I find the support to go on smiling in my sadness, his love makes me strong. Because he is at the forefront of the needs of my children, I am able to breathe and life is not so painful, I also know that if you, dear Mamita (of mine), needed anything, Fabrice would be there for you, as he has always been for me. I know that Fab is concerned about where Mela is living and where Loli is living. And so, I worry less. I am so proud of how he has fought for me. I have listened to him on the radio a number of times and how tightly I have hugged him in my heart at every word when his voice breaks, making me weep inside, so that nobody shall take notice. Thank you, my Fab for being so sublime.

For my Astrica, there is so much that I don't know where to begin. For instance, I want to tell her that her curriculum vitae saved me during the first year of my captivity, during the year of mourning for my Papá. I know that only she can understand what Papá's death meant to me. My consolation will always be that she was at his side, and through her I was, too. I need so badly to talk to her about all those moments, to hug her and cry till the well of tears I have in my body gives out. She is there as a point of reference in all that I do during the day. I always think: "I did this with Astrid when we were kids," or "Astrid did this better than me," or "If only Astrid were here," or "Thank God, Astrid isn't here to see this; she would have died of disgust" or of "terror," and, so on. How I now understand so many of those reactions that she had, things she didn't like or couldn't stand. How well I now understand her when she was annoyed with me for my attitudes or expressions. Now, I understand so many things about my Astrica and feel so close to and joined to her. I've heard her several times over the radio. I admire her so much for her impeccable expressiveness, the quality of her thought, her command over her emotions, the elegance of her sentiments. I listen to her and think, "I want to be like that." I have always considered her intellectually very superior to me. But, in addition, I have discovered that over these years a wisdom has grown in her that radiates as she speaks. I spend the whole day giving thanks to God for all of this. I know how much I owe to her and to Daniel. You cannot imagine my happiness when I learned that they had gotten married! I know that, like me in the jungle, Papá in heaven is happy. Daniel is a very special human being; if I had been asked I would have wanted him as Astrid's husband, the "adopted papá" of Anastasia and Stanis, and my brother-in-law. I like his intelligence, his generosity, and his prudence. Those three qualities are rarely to be found together and when they do appear they deserve admiration and respect. That is what I feel for Daniel—admiration and respect. What a beautiful family. God does things well. I can imagine the pleasure they must take in Anastasia and Stanis. I love them so much it kills me . . . how painful that their drawings were taken away from me! Anastasia's poem said, "by a stroke of luck, by a stroke of magic, or by a stroke of God, you will be back with us in three years or three days." And Stanis's drawing was a rescue by helicopter, I asleep in a little cove just like these here, and he was my rescuer. I adore my two little ones as if they were my own children. Besides, Anastasia is just like me, although I believe she is now a better horsewoman. I want to attend classes with her at L'Ecole Militaire. And Stanis, because he is my godson, I must take him to eat lots of ice cream at the Champs Elysées! What divine children. Enjoy them, Astrid, each age is a poem that never repeats. Take photographs of them, record a video, or a DVD I guess! I am now so behind the times in technology. Do it so that one day I will be able to see their different ages. And I remember Stanis poking the tip of the plastic sword from his Musketeer costume in my eye and my Papá amused by the incident celebrating the prank. Heartfelt treasures. I miss them so very, very, very much.

To Juanqui, where are you? I hear you only once in a while. I like it when he sends messages, he always tells me about the children and he knows that is pure happiness for me. But I am aware of how cruel and difficult this separation is. I understand everything and I keep loving him like that day we were stretched out on the beach counting the shooting stars. Tell him to be at peace with himself and me, that if life gives us the chance, we will come out fortified from this test.

I want to tell my Aunt Nancy that I have her with me always in my mind and my heart. That the best she did for me was to be at your side. That I have prayed to God to give me the opportunity to show her how much I love her, how much I feel she is mine, like another real mother that she is for me. And through her, I always send the energy of my love to all: Danilo, María Adelaída, Sebas and Tomás, Alix and Michael, Jonathan, Matthew and Andrew, adorable Pacho, Cuquín, and his sweetheart. I am happy that Pacho has returned to Colombia. How I would like to be there to help him in the beginning. Pedro will undoubtedly do it better than I would. And how I would have enjoyed being at that dinner with Toño! It has been like going back. I love all of them so much! I'm sure Pacho is going to do very, very well. I feel the good energy he sends with

"Nam-myoho-renge-kyo[12]."

Darling Mamita, there are so many people I would like to thank for remembering us, for not having abandoned us. For a long time, we have been the lepers that mar the ball, we captives are not a politically correct topic, it sounds better to say that people must stand up against the guerrillas even if some human lives are sacrificed. In the face of that, silence. Only time can clear consciences and elevate the spirit. I consider the greatness of the United States, for instance. That greatness is not merely the fruit of wealth alone in land, raw materials, etc., but the fruit of the greatness of spirit of the leaders who molded the nation. When Lincoln defended the right to life and the freedom of the black slaves of America, many Floridas and Praderas[13] had to be confronted. Many economic and political interests were considered more important than the life and liberty of a handful of blacks. But Lincoln was victorious, and today the priority of human life over economic and political interests has become part of the culture of that nation. In Colombia we must think of where we come from, who we are, and where we want to go. I aspire to our having that thirst for greatness one day that makes peoples rise up from nothingness to the sun. When we are unconditional vis-à-vis the defense of the life and liberty of our own, that is, when we are less individualistic and more committed to the common good, less indifferent and more involved, less intolerant and more compassionate, then at that time we will be the great nation that all of us would like to be. That greatness is there

12. Mantra of the practitioners of the Japanese school of Soka Gakkai, a form of Nichiren Buddhism.

13. FARC demands as a precondition for all negotiations that the municipalities of Florida and Pradera, in the department of Valle del Cauca, be demilitarized as a negotiation zone for exchanging hostages and prisoners.

asleep in our hearts. But hearts have hardened and weigh so heavily that no elevated sentiments are permitted.

But there are many people to whom I would like to give thanks for their contributions to arousing the spirit and the aggrandizement of Colombia. I cannot name them all but can account for some: President Alfonso López and, in general, the former liberal presidents. But especially to President López, because his death has been particularly painful for us. I have also regretted not having been able to embrace Hernán Echavarría, from whom I learned so much and to whom I owe so much. Let this be the moment for expressing my admiration and deep affection to the families of congressmen Juan Carlos Narvaez, Alberto Giraldo, Alberto Barraga, Alberto Quintero, Ramiro Echeverry, John Jairo Hoyos, and Edison Pérez. Every one of them is in my prayers, and I do not forget them even for a moment, as homage to the life that remains in me and belongs to them.

Mamita, they have come for the letters. I won't be able to cover all I would like to write. To Piedad and Chávez, all my affection and admiration. Our lives are there in their hearts, which I know to be big and valiant. To President Chávez, how much I would like to tell him so many things and, particularly, how much I appreciate his manner of being so spontaneous and generous when I listen to him on the radio in *Aló Presidente*. It moved me to listen when the *vallenato* children came to sing for him. It was a sublime moment of tenderness and brotherhood between Colombians and Venezuelans. Thank you for having taken an interest in this cause, which is ours, in which so little is spectacular, since when the pain of others becomes a statistic, nobody is interested. Thank you, President.

Thanks also to Álvaro Leyva. He was close, but the wars

waged against the freedom of a handful of forgotten ones are like a hurricane seeking to bring down everything. It is of no interest. His intelligence, his nobility, and his devotion have given pause to many, and here, more than the freedom of some poor crackpots chained up in the jungle, it is a matter of taking stock of what it means to defend human dignity. Thank you, Álvaro.

Thanks to Lucho Garzón for his commitment, his compassion, generosity, and devotion. Here, too, the fireflies lit up the jungle at the time of the concert. Here, too, we sang with the voice of hope.

Thanks to Gustavo Petro for remembering us with photos in the enclosure, and in his speeches, and every time he is able. The same goes for so many friends who help us with their declarations of support and encouragement, from Polo, from the Liberal Party. Thanks to all for not leaving us in oblivion, for not relegating us to the oblivion of the kidnapped.

I have heard Juan Gabriel Uribe several times contributing his enlightenment and knowledge in favor of the possibility of liberation. The same for Sahiel Hernández and Claudia López. Thank you.

Thanks and congratulations to the winners of the Bolivar Award, who have not deserted the cause of freedom. To Julio Sánchez Cristo, in particular. Thanks a thousand times for the commitment and the affection. I also give thanks to Daniel Coronel, for the warmth and devotion, and, to Juan Gabriel Uribe once more, for the constructive idea and the vast compassion for us.

It's just that we owe so much to the media. It is thanks to them that we have not gone mad in the lone solitude of the jungle. To Erwin Hoyos, congratulations for your prize and my constant and cumulative thanks for the *Voices of the Kidnapped* radio program, the thousands of hours of broadcasting messages from our families are equivalent to thousands of hours of relief from anguish and despair. God bless you.

The same goes to Nelson Moreno, Fernando Obando, Manuel Fernando Ochoa, and all the members of the *Carrilera de las 5* radio program. All of these endless years, we've found the strength to open our eyes thanks to the program's opening jingle, a happy prelude to the only remaining contact that we have with our families. May God grant us the possibility of hugging you one day and return a bit of the beneficent energy that fills your voices and our hearts every day of every month of every year of this terrible captivity.

Also, I would like to tell Dario Arizmendi that all of us here are aware of and grateful for your insistence in keeping memory of us alive. Thank you for continuing to stretch out your hand to us. Your voice is the only real force for coming out alive from here because it is the voice that protests and demands an accounting. Thank you, thank you!

To Juan Gassain, on so many occasions we've felt that he understands our suffering, takes it upon himself, feels it, and transmits it, making it possible for this test, which it has been our lot to undergo, to be alleviated by the company of millions of Colombians who then understand and share our feelings of frustration and desperation as well. In those friends of Todelar, in L. Guillermo Troya and all his group, we have encountered concern and commitment in moments of abandonment and solitude. They have always been there for us. Thank you.

I would like to name everybody but my time is up. Greetings to J.G. Rios and to so many others who have accompanied us all these years.

I don't want to say good-bye without sending a fraternal embrace to Monsignor Castro, as well as to Father Echeverry. They have been fighting for us constantly. They have spoken up for us always at a time when we are enveloped by a silence and abandonment beyond that of the jungle itself. May God enlighten and guide them so that we will soon be able to speak of all this as the past. But if not, if God should have other plans, we will see one another in heaven itself, giving thanks to God for His infinite pity.

My heart also belongs to France. And the "also" is redundant. *"Mon coeur appartient à la France, ma douce France qui m'a tant donné."* I write in Spanish so as not to draw attention that might impede delivery of this letter. When I think of God, and think of His blessing of all of us, I think of France. Providence seeks to express itself through channels of wisdom and love. Since the initiation of this kidnapping, France has had a voice of wisdom and love. It has never given up; it has never accepted the passing of time as the only solution, never faltered in defense of our right to be defended. When the night was at its darkest, France was the beacon. When the request for our freedom was disapproved, France did not keep silent. When our families were accused of harming Colombia, France gave them support and advice. I wouldn't believe it is possible to get out of here one day were it not for my knowledge of France's history and its people. I have prayed to God that I be granted the same power as that with which France has faced adversity so that I might feel worthy of being counted as one of her children. I love France from my soul, the roots of my being seeking to embed themselves within the elements of its national character, seeking always to be guided by principles, not interests. I love France with all my heart, for I admire the ability to mobilize a people who, like Camus, understand that to live is to commit oneself. Today, France has committed itself to the kidnapped of Colombia, as it has done with Aung San Suu Kyi and Anna Politkovskaya. It is always in search of justice, freedom, and truth. I love France because there is in France the elegance of being constant so it does not appear stubborn and the generosity of commitment so it does not fall into obsession. My unconditional and eternal love for France and the French people is the highest expression of my gratitude. I am not worthy of, nor do I deserve, the love they have bestowed upon me and I feel inadequate for even aspiring to the support of so many hearts. I am reassured by the thought that France's commitment is the commitment to another people who suffer, it is the right to aid other human beings in the face of pain and death, it is the decision to take action against the unacceptable, for all that has happened here is simply unacceptable.

President Chirac was with us for many years, ever firm, ever clear, ever compassionate. He and Dominique de Villepin are in my heart. All these years have been unbearable, but I do not believe that I would be able to stay alive without the commitment they have made to all of us in this living death here. President Sarkozy has taken the helm in profound changes for France. I am convinced that the power of his convictions and the nobility of these sentiments will open hearts and minds. I know that what we are living through is filled with unknowns, but history has its own schedule of maturation and President Sarkozy is poised on the meridian of history. With President Chávez and President Bush and the solidarity of the entire continent, a miracle for us is conceivable.

Over many years I have thought that as long as I live, as long as I breathe, I must keep up hope. I no longer have the same strength and it is now difficult for me to keep on believing, but I want them to know that what they have done for us has made the difference: they made us feel human.

My dearest Mamita, I would have other things to tell you. You know that I have had no news about Clara and her baby in a long time. Tell Pinchao to give you details; he will tell you the whole story. It is important that you evaluate what he explains and have the possibility of distancing yourself, being very prudent.

I know that you have been in touch with Marc Gonsalves's mother. He is a very special person, of great human quality. Tell her to send messages to him on the *Carrilera* program, which they listen to. I believe we all do. I am with another group, but I am very fond of Marc, so tell Jo that her son is all right.

And so, I don't want to say good-bye. God willing, this will reach you. You are deep in my soul, my loveliest Mamita. One final recommendation: financial matters (like premiums or such things)—have Astrid take care of them. I have also been thinking that if my apartment is empty and the payments aren't being paid, why don't you go there? That would be at least one worry less. If you want to discuss anything of a personal nature with me on the radio, tell it to me in French so that I understand what you are going to tell me about, and continue in Spanish. We could talk about "Uncle Jorge" for example, and I will understand. And so, Mamita, God will help us, guide us, give us patience, and shield us.

As always and forever, your daughter,

Ingrid Betancourt, 3:34 P.M.

LETTER FROM
MÉLANIE AND LORENZO

Darling Mama,

Your letter, your wonderful letter, has reached us after so many days of separation, of silence, of anticipation, of hope. It seems to come from worlds away–beyond space, beyond time–as if a lifetime has passed between us. Through all these years, I have searched for you everywhere, seeing you in my memories, through our struggles. Through all these years I have desperately tried to communicate with you, to find out whether you are alive. And suddenly, here you are–so near, so close to us. Reading your letter, I hear your voice again.

In the jungle where you are imprisoned, everything seems far away, even the sun. Everything hurts; everything is inhuman. Yet there could be nothing more true, more right, than the words you have found. Mama, you have woken us up. Your suffering is now our suffering, your despair is our urgency, your love and your courage is our strength. Today, I understand what it means to be free. We are so proud of you, Mama. As you suffer and struggle every day in humility, as you somehow still find strength enough to scorn your kidnappers' games, believe this: we are greater because of you. You have made us all greater.

You could not have written a better love letter to those dear to you. I snuggle up to the softness of your words and say to myself, over and over, "You are alive! You are alive!" But I also feel a great anxiety rising in me. Now that I sense you so near, I am afraid of losing you again. I have but one desire– to take you in my arms and say, "We are here, Mama. We are fighting to get you away from there. Listen to me. So many wonderful times are waiting for us. You will see us grow, see us accomplish so much, Loli and me." But I cannot see you, I cannot touch you, I cannot hold you or give you comfort. So I try to be prepared; I choose my words carefully; I make my voice calm and steady to convey all my strength and all my love through the messages I send to you over the radio.

I am so grateful to my grandmother, who from the first day has always been there, sending messages faithfully to you over the radio every night. Always, she has believed that you can hear us. Always, she has been steadfast.

Thanks to you, now the world can no longer plead ignorance. Your letter puts before us vividly what you and all the other hostages endure every day. No one now can deny that your plight is of the greatest urgency. Your letter is more than a testimony, more than an appeal: it is a great jolt. From your jungle prison, you have led the battle for liberty, liberty for all of us. If things change today, it will be thanks to you. I pray that your words keep FARC leader Manuel Marulanda and Colombian president Álvaro Uribe awake at night, unable to sleep until they acknowledge that, now, your lives are more important than their petty posturing. For myself, I can never again escape your words; wherever I go, they follow me, and I can no longer sleep until I have you beside me again.

In Colombia, your words have been a wake-up call to thousands of people; suddenly, after all these years, they realize that the hostages over there, buried deep in the jungle, are not only alive but are also people just like them, like all of us. I feel that thousands of people recognize themselves in your words, and are suddenly struck with the reality. Up to now, they've thought in numbers: so many hundred hostages, so many years spent in the jungle, so many people marching in protest, so many failed attempts at freedom. And suddenly you, with your courage, your strength, your intelligence, remind us of the obvious: you are simply a woman, a daughter, a mother. And with your words, you remind us that the other hostages, all of them, are also mothers and fathers, and daughters and sons, and sisters and brothers, with families waiting for them.

These days, I hope, we all know that there is no such thing as blind fate. We can no longer say, "There is no help for it, nothing can be done for these unhappy victims." No. Your life, all of our lives, our dreams, the happiness of that longed-for day when we can finally hold you in our arms—like the lives, the dreams, the happiness, of all the other hostages—in the end, it all depends on so few people: the leaders of FARC, the Colombian leaders with whom they demand negotiations. A handful of men, no more.

These men have no more excuses. They have had plenty of time to reflect on their actions; they have been able to weigh the options a thousand times. Are they still waiting for the perfect moment? Are they waiting for the best card to fall into their hands? Gamblers always believe they will soon draw the best card. But now the game is up. No more hands will be dealt. FARC must recognize that in the days and weeks to come, posterity's judgment of them hangs in the balance. If they choose to set out on the path toward freedom for the hostages, that decision will go down in the history books. If they prefer to wait, to play for time, to jockey for an advantage, hiding behind their prisoners like a shield, they will lose. Their loss will be great, and history also will remember it.

The Colombian president, from whom we could expect more compassion, humanity, or simply protection, through all of these years has shown nothing but indifference, or worse, time and again throwing forth new obstacles, hamstringing every attempt to reach an accord. Over and over again, we've run up against all the special interests that claim precedence over the lives of those we love, all the excuses—we must understand that the situation is complicated, we must be patient, and on and on. But once we admit that our first priority is to bring these people out of hell, the whole thing is simple: a group called FARC has been taking hostages, and negotiations must take place.

In your letter, you mention the United States, the struggle that Abraham Lincoln led for freedom, and the absurd obstacles he came up against. Just as absurd is the issue of Florida and Pradera, the two municipalities that FARC demands to have demilitarized as a precondition for negotiations. It seems insane, but it is still true that, for all these years, it has come down to this: a dispute about land. The negotiators hardly talk about methods of exchange; they are interested in nothing but the place where they will sit. Two square kilometers, more or less, where the negotiators can meet—this is the value set on the lives of our beloved! What ridiculous jockeying for power! I hope today that these equivocators can no longer pull the wool over our eyes, and that the government and FARC will be forced to face reality. The support that the Colombian government has refused us, we have found elsewhere—in Latin America, in Europe, and especially in France, which, as you say, is a country of high moral standing. The French president, Nicolas Sarkozy, has made your liberation a national priority, and is not giving up the fight. So many people are standing up to say that they will simply not accept the unacceptable, and will do anything to liberate you, you and the other hostages.

I wonder what you think about all of this, Mama, deep in the jungle, when you hear snatches of news on the radio. Perhaps you can no longer believe in a happy ending; perhaps you think it has dragged on too long, that too many hopes have been dashed. Me, I believe. But I know that this is bigger than me. From now on, all eyes will be turned toward you—eyes that reflect the world's outrage, consciences awakening, a movement growing to reach around the world. FARC must understand this: there will never be a better opportunity than today. The Colombian president must realize this: he has the power to rescue the hostages, to clear the way for you, Mama, and the others to return to their lives. Yes, he has the power. And perhaps this might be a great opportunity for him as well. Today, he can still save you. He can save all of you.

Mama, we know that this is urgent. We know that you are at the end of your rope. We can imagine how difficult it is to dredge up one last reserve of strength, to tackle, again and again, one more night of suffering, one more forced march into hell, one more humiliation. We know all this. We are going to get you out of there. In these terrible moments of doubt and defeat, say to yourself, I beg of you, that just a little farther on, beyond the jungle, we are here, we are thinking of you, we are fighting for you. A little farther, just a little farther, over the treetops, thousands of people are fighting ceaselessly for you, working to free you as soon as they can, because they recognize themselves in you, in your courage and your struggle, because they see you as one of their own—as a mother, a sister, a friend—and are determined not to let you down.

Your letter, your incredible words, have struck us like an electric shock. Heads of state have declared a state of emergency. The whole of Latin America is mobilized. The situation of the hostages in Colombia has become a major international issue. Your letter has put you in the spotlight, and no one can ignore you anymore.

You are worried about us, your children—Loli, Sebastián, and me. Mama, don't worry about us. We are fighting, we are awaiting your return; but we are living as well. We want you to be proud of us when you return. Your strength has always carried us. It is our turn now to carry you, to take care of you. It is time for Loli and me to give you what you have given us: the conviction that there is always still a bit more strength left when you think you have hit rock bottom. You are resilient, courageous, intelligent, and strong. I know that resilience, courage, and strength are not infinite. But we ask you for just a little bit more. Just a little bit more. You must hold on, Mama. Let our words, which come to you drip by drip over the radio, be your energy. Let our thoughts, which we send to you in secret, be your comfort. We will not forsake you, Mama. We will overcome. I want to see you again soon, see your smile again, feel your love of life. It will all seem new to you–the books, the laughter, and the lightness.

This is not a letter of farewell. This is a letter of reunion. See you soon, Mama.

Mélanie and Lorenzo

APPENDIX

A LIST OF FARC'S POLITICAL HOSTAGES

At the time of publication of this book, there are forty-four political hostages, among them Ingrid Betancourt. Two important hostages, Clara Rojas, Ingrid Betancourt's campaign director, and Colombian congresswoman Consuelo González, were liberated in January 2008, reviving hope for the rest.

The authors and editors of this work, as well as thousands of people who have mobilized across the world, call for the conclusion of humanitarian accords in the greatest urgency to exchange these forty-four hostages held by FARC for the five hundred guerrillas imprisoned by the government of Bogotá. The hostages are listed below, with the year of their kidnapping given in parentheses.

14 Military Personnel:

- Corporal Luis Arturo Arcia (1998)
- Corporal José Miguel Arteaga (1998)
- Corporal Luis Beltrán (1998)
- Lieutenant Juan Carlos Bermeo (1998)
- Sergeant Harvey Delgado (1998)
- Corporal Amaon Flórez (1998)
- Lieutenant Raimundo Malagón (1998)
- Corporal Libio Martínez (1997)
- Sergeant José Ricardo Marulanda (1998)
- Corporal Pablo Moncayo (1997)
- Sergeant Luis Moreno (1998)
- Corporal William Pérez (1998)
- Sergeant Erasmo Romero (1998)
- Corporal Róbinson Salcedo (1998)

19 Members of the Police Force:

- ▸ Corporal Julio Buitrago (1998)
- ▸ Sublieutenant Armando Castellanos (1999)
- ▸ Lieutenant William Donato (1998)
- ▸ Sublieutenant Carlos Duarte (1998)
- ▸ Captain Edgar Duarte (1998)
- ▸ Corporal Jhon Durán (1998)
- ▸ Sergeant Luis Erazo (1999)
- ▸ Sublieutenant Elkin Fernández (1998)
- ▸ Corporal José Libardo Forero (1999)
- ▸ Sergeant César Lasso (1998)
- ▸ Colonel Luis Mendieta (1998)
- ▸ Sublieutenant Álvaro Moreno (2000)
- ▸ Corporal Enrique Murillo (1998)
- ▸ Sublieutenant Luis Peña (1998)
- ▸ Sublieutenant Javier Rodríguez (1998)
- ▸ Sublieutenant Wilson Rojas (1998)
- ▸ Sublieutenant Jorge Romero (1998)
- ▸ Captain Guillermo Solarzano (2007)
- ▸ Sublieutenant Jorge Trujillo (1999)

8 Civilians / Political Figures:

- ▸ Orlando Beltrán (2001)
- ▸ Ingrid Betancourt (2002)
- ▸ Jorge Eduardo Gechen (2002)
- ▸ Alan Jara (2001)
- ▸ Oscar Lizcano (2000)
- ▸ Sigifredo López (2002)
- ▸ Luis Eladio Pérez (2001)
- ▸ Gloria Polanco (2001)

3 American Hostages:

- ▸ Thomas Howe (2003)
- ▸ Marc Gonsalves (2003)
- ▸ Keith Stannsen (2003)

Former Hostages:

Two civilians were liberated in January 2008, Clara Rojas (2/23/2002), and Consuelo González (9/10/2001), as well as little Emmanuel, son of Clara Rojas, born in captivity.

One hostage, Captain Julián Guevara, died while a prisoner in January 2006, after eight years in captivity.

Eleven hostages, representatives of the department of Valle del Cauca kidnapped in 2002, were executed on June 18, 2007, because of a supposed attack on the camp where they were held by FARC:

- ▸ Héctor Arismendi
- ▸ Carlos Barragán
- ▸ Carlos Charry
- ▸ Ramiro Echeverri
- ▸ Francisco Giraldo
- ▸ Jairo Hoyos
- ▸ Juan Carlos Narváez
- ▸ Nacianceno Orozco
- ▸ Edison Pérez
- ▸ Alberto Quintero
- ▸ Rufino Varelo

Another group of political hostages was assassinated by FARC on May 5, 2003, in Antioquia, near Medellín, during a rescue attempt by the army. These included Guillermo Gaviria Correa, ex-governor of Antioquia, and Gilberto Echeverri, former minister of defense, both captured on April 21, 2002, as well as eight military personnel, captured in 1999 in various operations:

- Samuel Ernesto Cote
- Héctor Lucuara
- Mario Alberto Marin
- Yercinio Navarrete
- Francisco Manuel Negrete
- Alejandro Ledesma Ortiz
- José Gregorio Pena
- Wagner Tapias Torres

3 Military Personnel Have Been Rescued:

- Antenor Biella
- Heriberto Aranguren Gonsalez
- Pedro Guarnizo Ovalle

2 Hostages Have Successfully Escaped:

- Sublieutenant John Pinchao, escaped on May 15, 2007, after nine years in captivity
- Fernando Araujo, escaped January 1, 2007, after six years in captivity; Araujo subsequently became minister of foreign affairs for the Uribe government.

LA LETTRE D'INGRID BETANCOURT

Jungle Colombienne,
mercredi 24 octobre
8h34

par un matin pluvieux, comme mon âme

Ma petite maman chérie adorée,

Tous les jours, je me lève en remerciant Dieu de t'avoir. Tous les jours, j'ouvre les yeux à 4 heures et je me prépare, afin d'être bien réveillée lorsque j'écouterai les messages de l'émission la *Carrilera de las 5*. Entendre ta voix, sentir ton amour, ta tendresse, ta confiance, ton engagement à ne pas me laisser seule, c'est mon espoir quotidien. Tous les jours, je demande à Dieu de te bénir, de te protéger et de me permettre un jour de pouvoir tout te rendre, te traiter comme une reine, à mes côtés, parce que je ne supporte pas l'idée d'être à nouveau séparée de toi.

Ici, la jungle est très épaisse, les rayons du soleil y pénètrent difficilement. Mais c'est un désert d'affection, de solidarité, de tendresse, et c'est la raison pour laquelle ta voix est le cordon ombilical qui me relie à la vie. Je rêve de t'embrasser si fort que je demeurerais incrustée en toi. Je rêve de pouvoir te dire « Maman, mamita, plus jamais tu ne pleureras pour moi, ni dans cette vie ni dans l'autre ». J'ai demandé à Dieu qu'il me permette un jour de te prouver tout ce que tu signifies pour moi, de pouvoir te protéger et de ne pas te laisser une seconde toute seule. Dans mes projets de vie, si un jour je retrouve la Liberté, je veux, mamita, que tu songes à vivre avec nous, ou avec moi. Plus jamais de messages, plus jamais de téléphone, plus jamais de distance, je ne veux plus qu'un seul mètre nous sépare, parce que je sais que tous peuvent vivre sans moi, sauf toi. Je me nourris chaque jour de l'espoir d'être ensemble, et nous verrons comment Dieu nous montrera la voie, comment nous nous organiserons, mais la première chose que je veux te dire, c'est que, sans toi, je n'aurais pas tenu jusque-là.

Tous les jours, tu me demandes comment est ma vie. Je sais que Pinchao t'a donné beaucoup de détails, et je le bénis et le remercie de t'avoir tout raconté. J'ai une grande admiration pour Pinchao. Ce qu'il a réussi est héroïque. Un jour, si Dieu le veut, je le serrerai très fort dans mes bras, ce que je n'ai pas pu faire quand il s'est évadé du campement. Aide-le autant que tu peux. Surtout s'il a besoin de demander l'asile. Dis-lui combien je l'aime et que j'ai prié Dieu pour qu'il survive à son exploit. Bon, depuis que Pinchao s'est évadé, nos conditions se sont encore détériorées. Les règles sont devenues draconiennes, et c'est terrible pour moi. Ils m'ont séparée de ceux avec qui je m'entendais le mieux, avec qui j'avais des affinités et pour qui j'éprouvais de l'affection, et ils m'ont mise dans un groupe humainement très difficile.

Mamita, je suis fatiguée, fatiguée de souffrir. J'ai été, ou j'ai tenté d'être forte. Ces six années de captivité, ou presque, m'ont démontré que je ne suis ni aussi résistante ni aussi courageuse, intelligente et forte que je le pensais. J'ai mené beaucoup de batailles, j'ai tenté de m'enfuir à plusieurs reprises, j'ai essayé de garder espoir comme on garde la tête hors de l'eau. Mais aujourd'hui, mamita, je me sens vaincue. Je voudrais penser qu'un jour je sortirai d'ici, mais je me rends compte que ce qui est arrivé aux députés, et qui m'a fait si mal, peut m'arriver à tout moment. Je pense que cela serait un soulagement pour tout le monde.

Je sens que mes enfants mènent une vie en suspens en attendant que je sois libre, et ta souffrance quotidienne, celle de tout le monde, fait que la mort m'apparaît comme une option douce. Rejoindre papa, dont je n'ai jamais achevé le deuil: tous les jours, depuis quatre ans, je pleure sa mort. Je crois toujours que je vais finir par m'arrêter de pleurer, que c'est désormais cicatrisé. Mais la douleur revient et se jette sur moi comme un chien déloyal, et de nouveau je sens mon cœur se briser en mille morceaux. Je suis fatiguée de souffrir, de porter cette douleur en moi chaque jour, de me mentir à moi-même en pensant que tout cela aura peut-être une fin, et de constater que chaque jour équivaut à l'enfer du précédent. Je pense à mes enfants, à mes trois enfants, à Sébastien, à Mela et à Loli. Tant de vie s'est écoulée entre nous, comme si la terre ferme était happée par la distance. Ils sont les mêmes et ne le sont plus. Chaque seconde de mon absence où je ne peux être là pour eux, pour soigner leurs blessures, pour les conseiller, leur donner de la force, de la patience et de l'humilité pour affronter la vie, toutes ces occasions perdues d'être leur maman empoisonnent mes moments d'infinie solitude, c'est comme si on m'injectait du cyanure dans les veines, goutte à goutte.

Mamita, c'est un moment très dur pour moi. Tout à coup, ils veulent des preuves de vie, et je t'écris, mon âme tendue sur ce papier. Je vais mal physiquement. Je ne mange plus, j'ai perdu l'appétit, mes cheveux tombent en grande quantité. Je n'ai envie de rien. Je crois que la seule bonne chose, c'est ça: n'avoir envie de rien. Car ici, dans cette jungle, l'unique réponse à tout est « Non ». Mieux vaut donc ne rien vouloir pour demeurer au moins libre de désirs. Cela fait trois ans que je demande un dictionnaire encyclopédique pour lire quelque chose, apprendre quelque chose, maintenir vive la curiosité intellectuelle. Je continue à espérer qu'au moins par compassion, ils m'en procureront un, mais il vaut mieux ne pas y penser. Ici, chaque chose est un miracle. Entendre ta voix chaque matin est un miracle, car ma radio est très vieille et abîmée. Essaie toujours de passer, comme tu le fais, en début d'émission, car, ensuite, il y a beaucoup d'interférences et à partir de 5h20 je ne peux que deviner ce que tu me dis. Et quand il y a une information importante (comme le mariage d'Astrid), répète-la au fil des messages. Je n'ai appris le mariage d'Astrid et de Daniel qu'il y a deux ans, à Noël. Tu me l'avais sûrement mentionné, mais, ce message, je ne l'avais pas entendu!!!

À propos de radio, je voudrais te demander, mamita chérie, de dire aux enfants que j'aimerais qu'ils m'envoient trois messages hebdomadaires, les lundis, mercredis et vendredis. Qu'ils t'envoient deux lignes sur ton e-mail et, toi, tu me les liras. Rien de transcendant, ce qui leur viendra à l'esprit ou ce qu'ils auront envie d'écrire en vitesse, du genre « Maman, aujourd'hui, il fait très beau, je vais déjeuner avec Maria, je l'aime beaucoup, je suis sûre qu'elle te plaira » ou « Je suis épuisée mais, aujourd'hui, j'ai appris plein de choses dans un cours que j'adore, sur les nouvelles techniques de cinéma ». Je n'ai besoin de rien d'autre, seulement d'être en contact avec eux. Chaque jour, j'attends avec impatience que tu parles d'eux ou que tu me dises si tu as parlé avec eux. C'est ce qui m'apporte le plus de joie, la seule chose qui réellement m'importe, la seule information vitale, transcendante, indispensable, le reste ne m'importe plus. Je voudrais que Sébastien m'écrive lui aussi. Je veux savoir où il en est de son travail, de sa vie affective, etc., etc. Je suis d'accord à 100% pour que tu ne m'appelles pas à l'aube, le dimanche. Je souffre beaucoup à l'idée que tu veilles toute la nuit, que tu attendes pendant des heures, que tu te fatigues... Je continue d'écouter l'émission par solidarité avec les autres, mais je serais plus tranquille de te savoir bien au chaud dans ton lit.

Bon, comme je te le disais, la vie ici n'est pas la vie, c'est un gaspillage lugubre du temps. Je vis ou survis dans un hamac tendu entre deux piquets, recouvert d'une moustiquaire et d'une tente qui fait office de toit et me permet de penser que j'ai une maison. J'ai une tablette où je mets mes affaires, c'est-à-dire mon sac à dos avec mes vêtements et la Bible, qui est mon seul luxe. Tout est prêt pour qu'on parte en courant. Ici rien n'est à soi, rien ne dure, l'incertitude et la précarité sont l'unique constante. À tout moment, ils peuvent donner l'ordre de faire son paquetage, et chacun doit dormir au fond de n'importe quel trou, étendu n'importe où, comme un animal. Ces moments sont particulièrement difficiles pour moi. Mes mains deviennent moites, mon esprit s'embrume, je finis par faire les choses deux fois plus lentement qu'à la normale. Les marches sont un calvaire car mon équipement est très lourd et j'arrive à peine à le porter. Parfois, les guérilleros me prennent certaines choses pour en alléger le poids mais me laissent « les pots », c'est-à-dire ce qui est nécessaire à notre toilette et qui est le plus lourd. Tout est stressant, je perds mes affaires ou ils me les confisquent, comme le jeans que Mela m'avait offert pour Noël, que je portais quand ils m'ont enlevée. Je ne l'ai plus jamais revu. L'unique chose que j'ai pu sauver, c'est la veste, et cela a été une bénédiction, car les nuits sont glaciales, et je n'avais rien d'autre pour me protéger du froid. Avant, j'adorais me baigner dans le fleuve. Comme je suis la seule femme du groupe, je dois y aller presque tout habillée: short, chemise, bottes! Comme nos petites grands-mères d'autrefois. Avant j'aimais nager dans le fleuve, mais maintenant je n'ai même plus le souffle pour le faire. Je suis faible, frileuse, je ressemble à un chat face à l'eau. Moi qui aimais tant l'eau, je ne me reconnais plus. Durant la journée, j'avais l'habitude de faire deux heures d'exercice, parfois trois. Je m'étais inventé un appareil, une sorte de petit banc fait avec des branches, que j'ai appelé step, en pensant aux exercices du gymnase: l'idée était de monter et descendre, comme s'il s'agissait d'une marche. Il avait l'avantage de prendre peu de place. Parce que, parfois, les campements sont si petits que les prisonniers sont pratiquement les uns sur les autres. Mais depuis qu'ils ont séparé les groupes, je n'ai ni l'envie ni l'énergie de faire quoi que ce soit. Je fais un peu d'étirements, car le stress me bloque le cou, et cela me fait très mal. Avec les exercices d'étirement, le split et le reste, je parviens à détendre un peu mon cou. Voilà toute mon activité, mamita. Je fais en sorte de rester silencieuse, je parle le moins possible pour éviter les problèmes. La présence d'une femme au milieu d'hommes qui sont prisonniers depuis huit ou dix ans est un problème. J'écoute RFI et la BBC, j'écris très peu parce que les cahiers s'accumulent et les porter est une vraie torture: j'ai dû en brûler au moins quatre. De plus, lors des inspections, ils nous prennent ce à quoi on tient le plus. Une lettre de toi qui m'était parvenue m'a été retirée après la dernière preuve de vie, en 2003. Les dessins d'Anastasia et de Stanis, les photos de Mela et de Loli, le scapulaire de papa, un programme de gouvernement en 190 points que j'avais annoté au fil des années, ils m'ont tout pris. Chaque jour, il me reste un peu moins de moi-même. Les autres détails t'ont été racontés par Pinchao. Tout est dur. C'est la réalité.

Il est important que je dédie ces lignes à ceux qui sont mon oxygène, ma vie. À ceux qui me maintiennent la tête hors de l'eau, qui ne me laissent pas couler dans l'oubli, le néant et le désespoir. Ce sont toi, mes enfants, Astrica et ses petits, Fab, Tante Nancy et Juanqui. À mes trois enfants, Sébastien, Mela et Loli, donne-leur avant tout ma bénédiction, qu'elle les accompagne à chaque pas. Chaque jour, je me confie à Dieu, Jésus et la Vierge. Je recommande mes enfants à Dieu afin que la foi les accompagne toujours et qu'ils ne s'écartent jamais de Lui. Dis-leur qu'ils ont toujours été une source de joie pendant cette captivité si dure. Ici, tout a deux visages, la joie se mêle à la douleur, le bonheur est triste, l'amour apaise et ouvre de nouvelles blessures; se souvenir, c'est vivre et mourir à nouveau.

Pendant des années, je n'ai pas pu penser aux enfants, parce que la douleur de la mort de papa absorbait toute ma capacité de résistance. Quand je pensais à eux, j'avais l'impression d'étouffer, je ne pouvais plus respirer. Alors, je me disais: « Fab est là, il veille à tout, il ne faut pas penser, il ne faut pas penser. » À la mort de papa, j'ai failli devenir folle. J'ai besoin de parler avec Astrica pour faire le deuil. Je n'ai jamais su comment cela s'est passé, qui était là, s'il m'a laissé un message, une lettre, sa bénédiction. Mais ce qui, au fil du temps, a soulagé mon tourment a été de penser qu'il est parti confiant en Dieu et qu'un jour je le serrerai à nouveau dans mes bras. J'en suis sûre. Mamita, te sentir forte à ce moment-là a été ma force. Je n'ai entendu des messages que lorsqu'ils m'ont mise dans le groupe de « Lucho » Eladio Pérez, le 22 août 2003, date anniversaire de sa fille Carope. Nous avons été de grands amis, ils nous ont séparés en août. Mais durant tout le temps passé ensemble, il a été mon soutien, mon protecteur, mon frère. Dis à Angela, Sergio, Laura, Marianita et à Carope que je les garde dans mon cœur, comme s'ils étaient de ma famille. À partir de cette date, j'ai écouté les messages que tu m'adresses avec une incroyable ténacité, jamais tu ne m'as fait défaut. Dieu te bénisse. Je te disais que, pendant des années, je n'ai pas pu penser aux enfants parce que je souffrais horriblement de ne pouvoir être avec eux. Aujourd'hui, je peux les entendre et ressentir plus de joie que de douleur. Je les cherche dans mes souvenirs, et je me nourris des images que j'ai gardées dans ma mémoire, à chacun de leurs âges. À chaque anniversaire, je leur chante « Happy Birthday » et je demande la permission de faire un gâteau. Auparavant, ils se montraient compréhensifs et je pouvais faire quelque chose. Mais depuis trois ans, lorsque je réitère ma demande, la réponse est non. Ça m'est égal. S'ils viennent avec un biscuit ou l'habituelle ration de riz et de haricots, je me figure que c'est un gâteau, et je fête leur anniversaire dans mon cœur. Je veux que vous sachiez que le 8 avril, le 6 septembre et le 1er octobre sont sacrés pour moi. Je fête aussi le 31 décembre, le 18 juillet, le 9 août, le 1er septembre, et aussi le 24 juin et le 31 octobre, dates anniversaire de Tante Nancy et de Pacho. J'espère ne pas m'être trompée.

À ma Mela, mon soleil de printemps, ma princesse de la constellation du Cygne, à elle que j'aime tant, je veux dire que je suis la maman la plus fière du monde. J'ai eu tellement de chance que Dieu me donne ces enfants, et ma Mela est le grand prix de ma vie. Quand elle avait cinq ans, elle me tenait déjà tête avec intelligence et affection, et depuis ce jour, j'ai une admiration sans bornes pour elle. Elle est pleine de sagesse et d'intelligence. Et si je devais mourir aujourd'hui, je partirais satisfaite de la vie, en remerciant Dieu pour mes enfants. Je suis heureuse pour son Master à New York. C'est exactement ce que je lui aurais conseillé. Le cinéma est sa passion, et je suis à 100% d'accord avec elle en tout. Mais, attention, il est très important qu'elle fasse son DOCTORAT. Dans le monde d'aujourd'hui, il faut des diplômes, même pour respirer. Faire son doctorat, c'est avoir d'autres aspirations, entrer dans un autre monde, plus exigeant, plus discipliné, c'est fréquenter les meilleurs parmi les meilleurs. Je ne me lasserai jamais d'insister auprès de Loli et de Mela pour qu'ils n'abandonnent pas avant d'avoir leur Ph-D. J'aimerais que Mela me le promette, qu'elle me promette de chercher sur Internet, dès maintenant, même si cela lui semble lointain, et de regarder les sites de Harvard, Stanford, Yale, etc., et de voir quels doctorats ils proposent. Dans la matière qui lui plaira, dans ce qui l'intéresse le plus, histoire, philosophie, archéologie, théologie, qu'elle cherche, rêve et s'enthousiasme, et en fasse sa mission personnelle. Je sais qu'elle veut travailler; tout le monde est chatouillé par l'envie de se mettre au travail, de commencer à produire quelque chose, de vouloir savoir qui on est en réalité, et cela doit faire partie de ses projets de vie. Plus on est fort, plus on y arrive, plus les occasions se présentent, plus grand est le monde auquel on aspire. Ma Mela, tu sais bien que tout cela est vital. J'ai trouvé formidable que tu fasses de la philo à la place de Sciences-Po. J'ai trouvé formidable que tu te sois mise à l'italien et au russe et, si l'occasion m'en est donnée, si la vie me le permet, j'essaierai de te rattraper. Je suis ton fan n°1, les mots me manquent pour te dire combien je valorise ton parcours, la lucidité de tes décisions, la maturité avec laquelle tu as choisi ta voie et la façon dont tu la suis. Je sais que l'école de cinéma où tu es inscrite est un must et je te tire mon chapeau. Je t'ai toujours dit que tu étais la meilleure, que tu es bien meilleure que moi, que tu es ce que j'aurais voulu être, mais en mieux. C'est pourquoi, forte de l'expérience que j'ai accumulée dans la vie et avec le recul que donne le monde vu à distance, je te demande, mon amour, de te préparer pour atteindre le sommet.

À mon Lorenzo, mon Loli Pop, mon ange de lumière, mon roi des eaux bleues, mon chief musician qui chante et m'enchante, au maître de mon cœur, je veux dire que depuis qu'il est né jusqu'au jour d'aujourd'hui, il a été la source de mes joies. Tout ce qui vient de lui est du baume pour mon cœur, tout me réconforte, tout m'apaise, tout me donne plaisir et tranquilité. C'est mon enfant chéri, mon petit bout de soleil. Comme j'ai envie de le voir, de l'embrasser, de le prendre dans mes bras et de l'entendre! Cette année, j'ai enfin pu entendre sa voix une ou deux fois. J'en ai tremblé d'émotion. C'est mon Loli, la voix de mon enfant, mais il y a une voix d'homme qui couvre cette voix d'enfant. Une grosse voix d'homme, rauque, comme celle de papa. Aurait-il aussi hérité de ses mains, ces grandes et belles mains qui me manquent tellement? Dieu m'aurait-il fait ce double cadeau? L'autre jour, j'ai découpé une photo dans un journal arrivé par hasard. C'est une publicité pour un parfum de Carolina Herrera, 212 Sexy Men. On y voit un jeune homme, et je me suis dit: « Mon Lorenzo doit être comme ça. » Et je l'ai gardée. Je t'aime tant, mon amour! Je me souviens du jour où tu as chanté sur la terrasse du Planetario, j'ai toujours su que tu avais une âme d'artiste et une voix d'ange. Je rends grâce à Dieu de savoir que tu joues de la guitare comme un dieu. Tu te souviens du professeur qui venait te donner des cours à la maison quand tu étais petit? Je te vois encore! J'étais toujours intriguée quand elle me disait que tu étais un très bon élève, alors que je ne t'entendais jamais jouer. Mais je me souviens de tes petits yeux qui brillaient quand la professeur arrivait ou quand elle s'en allait. Je m'en souviens tout le temps. De ça et de bien d'autres choses, mon cœur. J'ai tellement envie de me blottir contre toi et de dormir en te serrant contre moi, comme on le faisait avant qu'ils ne m'enlèvent. J'ai tellement envie de te couvrir de baisers. Et de t'entendre. De parler avec toi pendant des heures et que tu me racontes tout; et que, moi, je te raconte tout. J'ai su que tu avais eu 13,75 au bac. Tu as fait mieux que moi. Comme je suis fière de toi, mon cœur, de ton double diplôme en droit et en économie à la Sorbonne. Excellent. Je suis ravie. Je pense que tu ne devrais pas écarter Sciences-Po. Ce sont les mêmes matières, surtout si tu choisis la section éco-fi. Penses-y, tu pourrais te présenter à l'examen en septembre 2008, avec derrière toi un an de Sorbonne. C'est une école prestigieuse, qui t'ouvrira toutes les portes. Et tu peux réussir, tu es brillant. Une chose encore: ne néglige pas la musique. Tu as ça dans tes gènes. Et comme pour Mela, j'insiste, Master et Ph-D. Vous avez la vie devant vous, cherchez à vous hisser le plus haut possible. Étudier, c'est grandir: non seulement parce qu'on apprend, mais aussi parce que c'est une expérience humaine, parce qu'autour de vous, les gens vous enrichissent émotionnellement, en vous obligeant à un plus grand contrôle de soi, et spirituellement, en vous modelant un caractère au service d'autrui, où l'ego se réduit à sa plus minime expression et laisse la place à l'humilité et à la force morale. L'un ne va pas sans l'autre. C'est cela vivre: grandir pour être au service des autres. Voilà pourquoi ta musique est si importante. Grâce à elle, tu peux apporter bonheur, compassion, solidarité, engagement. Et grâce à tes études, tu pourras comprendre comment fonctionne notre société, ses codes, ses règles et trouver les solutions pour parvenir à un monde meilleur. À tous les deux, je vous dis la même chose: je suis trop heureuse d'être la maman d'êtres humains aussi formidables, qui m'émerveillent tellement. Je suis à 100% avec toi, mon cœur. Avec toi pour tout, et pour tout ce que tu voudras. Oui, je suis ta fan n°1, et j'ai même découpé la photo de mon idole, comme une adolescente! Merci de me donner tant de bonheur.

À mon Sébastien adoré, mon Babou bleu, mon petit prince des voyages astraux et ancestraux, j'ai tellement de choses à dire! Première-ment, que je ne veux pas quitter ce monde sans qu'il ne soit sûr et certain et n'ait la conviction absolue que ce ne sont pas deux, mais trois enfants chéris que Dieu m'a donnés et qu'ils sont inscrits comme tels sur le registre de la vie. Je le porte en moi, tous les jours, je me souviens de lui tel que je l'ai vu la première fois, déguisé en Zorro, il avait cinq ans et ses petits yeux bleus découvraient un monde qui changeait trop vite. Je voudrais parler des heures avec lui, comme je voudrais parler des heures avec ma Mela et des heures avec mon Loli. Mais avec lui, il me faudra dénouer des années de silence qui me pèsent trop depuis ma captivité. J'ai décidé que ma couleur favorite était le bleu de ses yeux, avec une touche du mauve clair du paréo dont il m'a fait cadeau, il y a de cela des années, aux Seychelles. Je m'habillerai de mauve clair quand je quitterai le vert-prison de cette jungle. Je veux qu'il m'apprenne à danser le moonwalk, je veux apprendre tant de choses de lui. Mais par-dessus tout, je veux qu'il sache que je pense qu'il est très beau, comme sa maman, très intelligent, comme son papa, et qu'il possède mon caractère, ce qui parfois peut être un avantage. Mais en général, c'est un grand Karma. C'est pourquoi chaque fois que je pense à toi, mon cœur, je ris de nous deux, je ris de toi et je ris de moi. Nous avons tourné en rond pour arriver exactement là où nous avions commencé: nous nous aimons de toute notre âme. Oui, mon Babou, il faut que je te parle, pour te demander pardon pour tous ces moments où je n'ai pas été à la hauteur, pardon pour mon manque de maturité alors que je devais te protéger et te draper dans mon amour et te donner des forces pour la vie. Pardon de ne pas avoir osé aller vers toi et te dire que tout peut changer, sauf mon amour pour toi. Je t'écris tout cela pour que tu le gardes dans ton âme, mon Babou adoré, au cas où je ne parviendrais pas à sortir d'ici, et pour que tu comprennes ce que j'ai compris quand ton frère et ta sœur sont nés: je t'ai toujours aimé comme le fils que tu es et que Dieu m'a donné. Le reste n'est que formalités.

À présent, là, tout de suite, il me faut parler de mon Fab. Comment ne pas lui dire que nos enfants sont mon bonheur. Que les moments les plus heureux de ma vie portent la marque de son amour, de sa présence, de sa personnalité, de sa vitalité, nos enfants sont lumineux. Comme l'a dit papa à Astrid et à moi, « ce sont des splendeurs »!! Et je m'adresse à Fab parce que c'est à lui que je dois tout cela: ma vie nouée au fil de cet amour inconditionnel qui ne s'est jamais rompu, de ce serment éternel que nous nous sommes fait à Monguí de nous aimer par-dessus tout et que nous n'avons jamais brisé. Seul l'amour peut expliquer ce que nous sommes, lui et moi. Il ne s'agit ni de conventions ni des rituels du monde, mais de l'esprit de l'amour de Dieu, qui donne tout sans condition. Je sais que Fab a beaucoup souffert à cause de moi. Mais que sa souffrance soit soulagée en sachant qu'il a été une source de paix pour moi. Dieu nous a envoyé cette épreuve afin que nous en sortions grandis, que nous soyons humainement meilleurs et que nous écartions tout ce qui est inutile et encombre l'âme. Ce chemin nous le faisons ensemble, même si nous sommes séparés, et nos efforts, notre combat, sont comme une lumière pour nos enfants. Fab est ma plus grande consolation; parce qu'il est là, je sais que mes enfants vont bien, et s'ils vont bien, le reste n'est pas grave. Dis-lui que je me repose sur lui, que je pleure sur son épaule, que je m'appuie sur lui pour continuer à sourire de tristesse, et que son amour me rend forte. Parce qu'il fait face aux besoins de mes enfants, je peux cesser de respirer sans que la vie ne me fasse trop mal. Mamita, je sais aussi que si tu as besoin de quoi que ce soit, Fabrice sera là pour toi comme il l'a toujours été pour moi, je sais que Fab s'occupe de l'endroit où vit Mela et de l'endroit où vit Loli. Alors je m'angoisse moins. Je suis si fière de la manière dont il se bat pour moi. Plusieurs fois je l'ai entendu à la radio, et je l'ai embrassé du fond du cœur à chacun de ses mots quand sa voix se brisait et quand je pleurais en mon for intérieur pour que personne ne le remarque. Merci, mon Fab, tu es merveilleux.

À mon Astrica, tant de choses, que je ne sais par où commencer. Tout d'abord, lui dire que « sa feuille de vie » m'a sauvée pendant la première année de captivité, pendant l'année du deuil de papa. Elle seule peut comprendre ce que la mort de papa a signifié pour moi. Ma consolation sera toujours de savoir qu'elle était à ses côtés et qu'à travers elle, je l'étais aussi. J'ai tant besoin de parler avec elle de tous ces moments, de la prendre dans mes bras et de pleurer jusqu'à ce que se tarisse le puits de larmes qu'est mon cœur. Elle est un exemple pour tout ce que je fais dans la journée. Je pense toujours: « Ça, je le faisais avec Astrid quand nous étions petites » ou: « Ça, Astrid le faisait mieux que moi ». Ou: « Si Astrid était là. » Ou: « Dieu merci, Astrid n'a pas vu ça, elle en serait morte de dégoût ou de peur », etc. Comme je comprends à présent ses réactions, quand il y avait des choses qu'elle n'aimait pas ou qu'elle ne supportait pas. Comme je comprends maintenant que mes mots ou mon comportement aient pu l'agacer. Je comprends tellement mon Astrica et je me sens si près, tout près d'elle. Je l'ai entendue plusieurs fois à la radio. Je ressens beaucoup d'admiration pour sa façon impeccable de s'exprimer, pour la qualité de ses réflexions, pour la maîtrise de ses émotions, pour l'élégance de ses sentiments. Je l'entends et je pense: « Je veux être comme ça. » J'ai toujours pensé qu'elle était très supérieure à moi intellectuellement. Et de plus, au long de toutes ces années, j'ai découvert la sagesse qui émane d'elle et rayonne quand elle parle. Voilà pourquoi je n'ai de cesse de remercier Dieu. Je sais que je lui dois beaucoup, à elle et à Daniel. Vous ne pouvez imaginer comme j'ai été heureuse quand j'ai appris qu'elle s'était mariée. Je sais que, là-haut, papa est heureux, comme moi dans cette jungle. Pour moi, Daniel est un être à part, et si on m'avait demandé mon avis, j'aurais voulu que ce soit lui le mari d'Astrid, le « papa adoptif » d'Anastasia et de Stanis, lui, mon beau-frère. J'aime son intelligence, sa bonté et sa prudence. Ces trois qualités sont rarement réunies chez une personne mais, quand c'est le cas, elles forcent l'admiration et le respect. J'ai de l'admiration et du respect pour Daniel. Quelle merveilleuse famille, Dieu fait bien les choses. J'imagine qu'ils profitent d'Anastasia et de Stanis… Ça m'a fait très mal qu'on me confisque leurs dessins. Le poème d'Anastasia disait: « Par un tour de force, un tour de magie ou un tour du bon Dieu, dans trois ans ou dans trois jours, tu seras de retour parmi nous. » Et le dessin de Stanis représentait un sauvetage en hélicoptère, moi endormie dans une cachette identique à celles d'ici, et lui en sauveur. J'adore mes deux petits comme mes propres enfants. Aussi parce qu'Anastasia me ressemble, même si elle monte beaucoup mieux à cheval que moi. Je veux prendre des cours avec elle à l'École militaire. Et parce que Stanis est mon filleul et que je dois l'emmener manger une glace sur les Champs-Élysées. Quels enfants merveilleux! Profites-en, Astrid, chaque âge est un poème qui s'efface une fois lu. Prends des photos, fais des vidéos, je devrais dire des DVD. En matière de technologie, j'ai du retard. Fais-le, afin qu'un jour je puisse les voir à des âges différents. Je me souviens de Stanis, déguisé en mousquetaire, qui me mettait la pointe de son épée dans l'œil, et de papa qui était heureux comme tout de fêter ses pitreries. Ce sont des trésors chers à mon cœur. Ils me manquent beaucoup, beaucoup, beaucoup.

À Juanqui: « Où es-tu? » Je ne l'entends que de temps en temps. J'aime qu'il m'envoie des messages, qu'il me parle des enfants et ça, il le sait, c'est un pur bonheur pour moi. Je sais que cette séparation est cruelle et difficile, je comprends tout et je l'aime comme le jour où nous avons compté les étoiles filantes, allongés sur la plage. Dis-lui qu'il soit en paix avec lui-même et avec moi. Que si la vie nous le permet, nous sortirons de cette épreuve encore plus forts qu'avant.

Je voudrais dire à Tante Nancy que je pense constamment à elle et que je la porte dans mon cœur. Être à tes côtés est ce qu'elle a fait de mieux pour moi. Je prie pour avoir l'occasion de lui prouver que je l'aime, que je la sens mienne, qu'elle est pour moi une autre maman. À travers elle, j'envoie tout mon amour à tous et à toutes: Danilo, Maria Adelaída, Sebás et Tomás, Alix et Michael, Jonathan, Matthew et Andrew, Pacho, Cuquín et sa fiancée. Je suis contente que Pacho soit rentré en Colombie. Comme j'aimerais être là pour l'aider à démarrer. Pedro le fera sans aucun doute beaucoup mieux que je n'aurais pu le faire. Et comme j'aurais aimé assister à ce repas avec Toño. Ce devait être comme un retour en arrière. Je les aime tous tellement. Je suis certaine que pour Pacho tout va aller très bien. Je reçois toute l'énergie qu'il m'envoie avec « Nam-myoho-renge-kyo ».

Mamita, il y a tant de gens que je voudrais remercier de se souvenir de nous, de ne pas nous avoir abandonnés. Pendant longtemps, nous avons été comme les lépreux qui gâchent la fête. Les otages ne sont pas un sujet « politiquement correct », cela sonne mieux de dire qu'il faut être fort face à la guérilla, quitte à sacrifier quelques vies humaines. Face à cela, le silence. Seul le temps peut réveiller les consciences et élever les esprits. Je pense à la grandeur des États-Unis, par exemple. Cette grandeur n'est pas le fruit de la richesse de la terre ou des matières premières, etc., mais celui de la grandeur d'âme des dirigeants qui ont modelé cette nation. Quand Lincoln a défendu le droit à la vie et à la liberté des esclaves noirs en Amérique, il a dû faire face à des problèmes comme ceux de Florida et de Pradera, s'opposer à des intérêts économiques et politiques que d'aucuns considéraient plus importants que la vie et la liberté d'une poignée de Noirs. Mais Lincoln a gagné et, aujourd'hui, la priorité de la vie humaine sur tout intérêt économique et politique fait partie de la culture de cette nation. En Colombie, nous devons encore penser à nos origines, à ce que nous sommes et où nous voulons aller. Moi, j'aspire à ce qu'un jour nous ayons cette soif de grandeur qui fait surgir les peuples du néant et les propulse vers le soleil. Le jour où nous défendrons la vie et la liberté des nôtres sans faire de concession aucune, c'est-à-dire quand nous serons moins individualistes et plus solidaires, moins indifférents et plus engagés, moins intolérants et plus compatissants, alors, ce jour-là, nous serons la grande nation que nous appelons tous de nos vœux. Cette grandeur est là, endormie dans les cœurs. Mais les cœurs se sont endurcis et pèsent si lourd qu'ils ne nous permettent pas d'élever nos sentiments.

Il y a pourtant beaucoup de gens que je voudrais remercier car ils ont contribué à réveiller les esprits et à faire grandir la Colombie. Je ne peux pas tous les mentionner, mais je citerai le président Alfonso Lopez et en général tous les présidents libéraux. Le président Lopez parce que sa mort a été pour nous une grande douleur. Je regrette aussi de ne plus pouvoir embrasser Hernan Echevarría, qui m'a tant appris et à qui je dois tant; que ce soit ici l'occasion d'exprimer mon admiration et ma profonde affection aux familles des députés, Juan Carlos Narvaez, Alberto Giraldo, Alberto Barraga, Alberto Quintero, Ramiro Echeverry, John Jairo Hoyos, Edinson Pérez. Je prie pour chacun d'eux, je ne les oublie pas, en hommage à la vie qui est en moi et qui leur appartient.

Mamita, hélas, ils viennent ramasser les lettres. Je ne vais pas pouvoir écrire tout ce que je voudrais. À Piedad et à Chavez, toute, toute mon affection et mon admiration. Nos vies sont là, dans leur cœur, que je sais grand et valeureux. Je voudrais dire tant de choses au président Chavez, combien j'aime sa spontanéité et sa générosité quand je l'entends à la radio dans l'émission *Aló Presidente*. Les enfants qui ont chanté pour lui des vallenatos m'ont émue, c'était un merveilleux moment de tendresse et de fraternité entre Colombiens et Vénézuéliens. Je le remercie de s'intéresser à notre cause, qui attire si peu l'attention, parce que la douleur d'autrui n'intéresse personne quand elle fait partie des statistiques. Merci Monsieur le Président.

Merci également à Alvaro Leyva. Il était proche de réussir, mais les guerres contre la liberté de cette poignée d'oubliés sont comme un ouragan qui arrache tout sur son passage. Elles n'intéressent personne. Son intelligence, sa noblesse, sa constance en ont fait réfléchir plus d'un et, ici, il s'agit moins de la liberté de quelques pauvres fous prisonniers dans la jungle que de prendre conscience de ce que signifie défendre la dignité humaine. Merci Alvaro.

Merci à Lucho Garzón pour son engagement, sa compassion, sa générosité et sa constance. Ici aussi, les lucioles éclairent la forêt à l'heure d'un concert. Ici aussi, nous chantons avec la voix de l'espérance.

Merci à Gustavo Petro pour s'être souvenu de nous en affichant des photos, en prononçant des discours chaque fois qu'il le peut. Merci à tous les amis qui nous aident par leurs déclarations de soutien, au Polo, du Parti libéral. Merci à tous de ne pas nous laisser dans l'oubli, de refuser qu'on oublie les otages.

J'ai entendu à plusieurs reprises Juan Gabriel Uribe mettre ses connaissances et son intelligence au service d'une possible libération. De même à Sahiel Hernández et à Claudia López. Merci.

Merci et bravo à ceux qui ont reçu le prix Bolívar, et n'ont jamais cessé de défendre la cause de la liberté. En particulier, merci à Julio Sánchez Cristo pour son engagement et sa tendresse. Merci à Daniel Coronel pour son courage et sa constance et merci encore à Juan Gabriel Uribe pour ses réflexions constructives et son immense compassion.

Nous devons beaucoup aux médias. Grâce à eux, nous ne sommes pas devenus fous dans la solitude de la jungle. Mes félicitations à Erwin Hoyos pour son prix, et mes remerciements et mon admiration pour son émission *Las Voces del Secuestro*, dont les milliers d'heures passées à transmettre les messages de nos familles ont été pour nous des milliers d'heures sans angoisse ni désespoir. Que Dieu le bénisse.

Merci à Nelson Bravo, Hernando Obando, Manuel Fernando Ochoa et à l'équipe la *Carrilera de las 5*. Tout au long de ces interminables années, nous avons eu la force de garder les yeux grands ouverts grâce au jingle de l'émission, heureux prélude au seul contact qui nous reste avec nos familles. Que Dieu nous donne un jour la possibilité de les embrasser et de leur rendre une partie de l'énergie que leur voix a inoculée dans nos cœurs, chaque jour de chaque mois de chaque année de cette terrible captivité.

Je voudrais dire aussi à Dario Arizmendi qu'ici nous sommes tous conscients de son obstination à faire en sorte que notre souvenir demeure vivant, et que nous l'en remercions. Merci de continuer à nous tendre la main. Sa voix est la seule véritable force qui nous permettra de sortir d'ici vivants, car c'est la voix qui demande des comptes. Merci, merci.

Combien de fois n'avons-nous pas senti que Juan Gassain comprenait notre souffrance, l'avait faite sienne et avait rendu cette épreuve plus légère grâce à la compagnie de milliers de Colombiens qui, eux aussi, comprennent et partagent notre sentiment de frustration et de désespoir. Dans les moments de solitude et d'abandon, nous avons senti l'intérêt et l'engagement des amis de Todelar, de L. Guillermo Troya et de toute son équipe. Ils ont toujours été là pour nous. Merci.

Je voudrais nommer tout le monde, mais je n'en ai plus le temps. Bonjour à J. G. Rios et à tous ceux qui nous ont accompagnés pendant toutes ces années.

Je ne voudrais pas terminer cette lettre sans envoyer un fraternel salut à monseigneur Castro et au père Echeverry. Ils se sont toujours battus pour nous. Ils ont toujours pris la parole quand le silence et l'oubli nous recouvraient plus que la jungle elle-même. Que Dieu les guide afin que très vite nous puissions parler de tout cela au passé. Et sinon, si Dieu en décide autrement, nous nous retrouverons au ciel et nous le remercierons pour son infinie miséricorde.

Mon cœur appartient aussi à la France. Et le « aussi » est de trop. Ma douce France qui m'a tant donné*. Je dois revenir à l'espagnol pour ne pas créer des suspicions qui rendraient difficile l'acheminement de cette lettre. Quand je pense à Dieu, quand je pense qu'il nous bénit tous, je pense à la France. La Providence s'exprime par la sagesse et l'amour. Depuis le début de mon enlèvement, la France a été la voix de la sagesse et de l'amour. Elle ne s'est jamais avouée vaincue, elle n'a jamais accepté le passage du temps comme unique solution. Elle n'a jamais vacillé dans la défense de nos droits. Dans la nuit la plus noire, la France a été un phare. Quand il était mal vu de demander notre liberté, la France ne s'est pas tue. Quand ils ont accusé nos familles de faire du mal à la Colombie, la France les a soutenues et consolées.

Je n'arriverais pas à croire que nous pourrons recouvrer un jour la liberté si je ne connaissais pas l'histoire de la France et de son peuple. J'ai demandé à Dieu qu'il m'insuffle la même force que celle avec laquelle la France a su supporter l'adversité, afin de me sentir plus digne d'être comptée parmi ses enfants. J'aime la France de toute mon âme, les racines de mon être cherchent à se nourrir des composantes de son caractère national, guidé par les principes et non par les intérêts. J'aime la France de toute mon âme, car j'admire ce peuple capable de se mobiliser car, comme le disait Camus, il sait que vivre, c'est s'engager. Aujourd'hui, la France s'est engagée aux côtés des otages de la jungle colombienne, comme elle l'a fait pour Aung San Suu Kyi ou pour Anna Politkovskaïa. Toujours en quête de justice, de liberté et de vérité. J'aime la France en toute lucidité, car elle est élégante dans sa constance afin de ne pas paraître opiniâtre, et généreuse dans ses engagements afin de ne pas sombrer dans l'obsession. Mon amour inconditionnel et éternel pour la France et pour le peuple français est l'expression de ma gratitude. Je ne suis pas digne, ni ne mérite l'attachement qu'il m'a témoigné, et je me sens bien peu de chose pour ne serait-ce qu'aspirer au soutien de tant de cœurs. Je me rassure en me disant que l'engagement de la France est celui d'un peuple pour un autre peuple qui souffre. C'est le droit d'aider d'autres êtres humains en proie à la douleur. C'est la décision d'agir face à l'inacceptable, parce que, en définitive, tout ce qui s'est passé ici est simplement inacceptable. Le président Chirac nous a accompagnés pendant des années. Toujours ferme, toujours clair, toujours plein de compassion. Lui et Dominique de Villepin, je les porte dans mon cœur. Toutes ces années ont été terribles, mais je crois que je ne serais plus en vie sans le soutien qu'ils nous ont apporté, à nous tous qui, ici, sommes des morts-vivants. Le président Sarkozy a décidé de profonds changements en France. Je suis persuadée que la force de ses convictions et la noblesse de ses sentiments éclaireront les cœurs et les esprits. Je sais que ce que nous vivons est plein d'incertitude, mais l'Histoire se fait selon un temps qui lui est propre. Et le président Sarkozy se tient sur le méridien de l'Histoire. Avec le président Chavez, le président Bush et la solidarité de tout le continent latino-américain, le miracle pourrait se produire. Pendant des années, j'ai pensé que tant que je serais en vie, tant que je respirerais, je garderais espoir. Je n'ai plus cette force, il m'est très difficile de continuer à croire, mais je veux que vous sachiez que ce que vous avez accompli pour nous a fait la différence. Nous nous sommes sentis des êtres humains. Merci.

Mamita, j'ai encore tant de choses à te dire. T'expliquer que je n'ai pas de nouvelles de Clara et de son bébé depuis longtemps. Demande à Pinchao qu'il te donne des détails, il te racontera tout. Il est important que tu accordes du crédit à ce qu'il te racontera et que tu aies la possibilité de prendre des distances. Je sais que tu as eu des contacts avec la maman de Marc Gonzalvez. C'est un être d'une grande qualité humaine. Dis à sa maman qu'elle lui envoie des messages par le biais de *Carrilera 5*: ils écoutent l'émission. Je crois que nous l'écoutons tous. Je suis maintenant avec un autre groupe, mais j'aime beaucoup Marc, et dis à Jo que son fils va bien.

Je ne veux pas te quitter. Dieu veuille que cette lettre te parvienne. Je te porte dans mon âme, ma petite mamita chérie. Une chose encore: qu'Astrid s'occupe de la partie économique (remise de prix ou autres choses du même genre). J'ai pensé aussi que puisque personne n'habite mon appartement, et que si on ne paye pas les traites, tu pourrais t'y installer. Ce serait un souci de moins. Si tu veux me dire quelque chose de personnel à la radio, dis-le en français afin que je comprenne de quoi il s'agit, et continue en espagnol, nous pourrions parler de « l'oncle Jorge » par exemple, et je comprendrai. Mamita, que Dieu nous vienne en aide, nous guide, nous donne la patience et nous protège.

Pour toujours et à jamais, ta fille,

Ingrid Betancourt, 15h34

LA CARTA DE INGRID BETANCOURT

Selvas de Colombia
miercoles 24 octobre
8:34

Mañana lluviosa, como mi alma

Mi mamita adorada y divina de mi alma,

Todos los días me levanto dándole gracias a Dios por tenerte. Todos los días abro los ojos a las 4 :a m y me preparo para estar bien despierta para oír tu mensaje en la *Carrilera de las 5*. Esa es mi ilusión diaria, oír tu voz, sentir tu amor, tu ternura, tu constancia y entrega en el compromiso de no dejarme sola. Todos los días le pido a Dios que te bendiga, te cuide, te proteja, y me permita algun día tener la oportunidad de consentirte en todo, darte gusto en todo, tenerte como una Reina al lado mío ; porque no soporto la idea de volverme a separar de ti. Esta es una selva muy tupida, dificílmente entran los rayos del sol. Pero es desierta en afecto, solidaridad o ternura. Por eso tu voz es mi cordón ombilical con la vida. Sueño con abrazarte tan fuerte que quede incrustada en ti. Sueño con decirte « Mamita, nunca más en esta vida o en la otra, volverás a llorar por mi ». Porque le he pedido mucho a Dios que me permita demostrarte todo lo que significas para mi, y cuidarte y no dejarte un instante sola. En mis planes de vida, si llega algun día la Libertad, quiero Mamita, que pienses en vivir con nosotros – o conmigo-. No más mensajes ; no más teléfonos, no más distancias, no quiero que exista ni un metro de distancia entre tu y yo. Porque sé que todos pueden vivir sin mi, menos tu. De esa ilusión de las dos, me nutro a diario, ya veremos como Dios abre caminos y nos organisaremos. Pero lo primero que que quería decirte es que sin ti, no hubiera aguantado hasta hoy.

A diario me preguntas como es mi vida. Yo sé que Pinchao te dió muchos detalles y le bendigo y le agradezco por haberte contado todo. Siento gran admiración por Pinchao. Lo que logró es algo heróico. Algun día, si Dios quiere, le daré un tremendo abrazo, como aquel que no pude darle cuando se fue del campamento. Ayudale en todo lo que puedas, sobre todo si necesita asilarse. Díle cuanto lo quiero y las gracias que le he dado a Dios de que saliera vivo de su hazaña. Bien, las cosas desde la fuga de Pinchao se endurecieron para nosotros. Las medidas se extremaron y eso ha sido terrible para mi. Me separaron de las personas con las cuales me entendía, con las cuales tenía afinidades y afecto y me pusieron en un grupo humano muy dificil. Estoy, Mamita, cansada, cansada de sufrir. He sido, o tratado de ser fuerte. Estos casi seis años de cautiverio han demostrado que no soy tan resistente, ni tan valiente, ni tan inteligente, ni tan fuerte como yo creía. He dado muchas batallas, he tratado de escaparme en varias oportunidades, he tratado de mantener la esperanza como quien mantiene la cabeza fuera del agua. Pero Mamita, ya me doy por vencida. Quisiera pensar que algun día saldré de aqui, pero me doy cuenta que lo de los diputados – que tanto me ha dolido- me puede pasar en cualquier momento. Pienso que eso sería un alivio para todos. Siento que mis niños estan con sus vidas en stand-by esperando que yo salga, y tu sufrimiento diario, y el de todos, hace que la muerte me parezca casi como una dulce opción. Estar con mi papito, cuyo duelo no termino de hacer, porque todos los días desde hace 4 años lloro su muerte. Siempre pienso qua ya al fin voy a dejar de llorar, que ya cicatrizó. Pero el dolor vuelve y se me echa encima como un perro traicionero, y vuelvo a sentir que se me despedaza el corazón. Estoy cansada de sufrir, de llevarlo por dentro todos los días, de decirme mentiras a mi misma, de que pronto esto va a terminar, y de ver que cada día es igual al in fierno del anterior. Pienso en mis niños, en mis 3 niños, en Sebastián, en Mela y en Loli. Tanta vida ha pasado entre nosotros, como si la tierra firme fuera desapareciendo en la distancia. Son los mismos y ya son otros, y cada segundo de mi ausencia, de no poder estar ahí para ellos, de curarle las heridas, de no poder aconsejarlos, o darles fuerza y paciencia y humildad ante los golpes de la vida, todas las oportunidades perdidas de ser su mamá, me envenenaron los momentos de infinita soledad como si me pusieran un suero de cianura por entre las venas. Mamita, este es un momento muy duro para mi. Piden pruebas de supervivencia a quemarropa, y aqui estoy escribiendote mi alma tendida sobre este papel. Estoy mal físicamente. No he vuelto a comer, el apetito se me bloqueó, el pelo se me cae en grandes cantidades, no tengo ganas de nada. Y creo que eso último es lo único que está bien. No tener ganas de nada. Porque aquí, en esta selva, la única respuesta a todo es « No ». Es mejor, entonces, no querer nada para quedar libre al menos de deseos. Hace tres años que estoy pidiendo un diccionario enciclopédico para leer algo, aprender algo, mantener la curiosidad intelectual viva. Sigo esperando que al menos por compasión me faciliten uno, pero es mejor no pensar en eso. De ahí para adelante, cualquier cosa es un milagro, hasta oírte por las mañanas porque el radio que tengo es muy viejo y dañado. Trata siempre de pasar como lo haces al principio del programa, ya después el radio coge muchas interferen-cias y a partir de las 5 :20 ya no puedo sino adivinar lo que estás diciendo. También, cuando haya información importante (como el matrimonio de Astrid) repítelo en varios mensajes. Yo no vine a enterarme de lo de As-trid y Daniel sino en la penúltima Navidad. Seguro lo habías mencionado y ese mensaje no lo oí.

Ahora quiero volver al tema de la radio. Quiero pedirte mamita linda que le digas a los niños que quiero que me manden 3 mensajes semanales, los lunes, los miércoles y los viernes. Que te manden dos renglones a tu correo internet y tu me los lees. Nada trascendental, sólo lo que puedan y se les ocurra escribir, estilo « Mamita, hoy está el día divino », « Voy a almorzar con María, la quiero mucho sé que te va a encantar » o « Estoy rendida, pero hoy aprendí mucho en una clase que me encanta de nuevas técnicas de filmación » No necesito nada más, pero sí necesito estar en contacto con ellos. De hecho cada día espero con anhelo a ver si vas a mencionarlos o si hablaste con ellos. Es lo que más me da felici-dad, es lo único que realmente me importa saber, es la única información vital, trascendental, imprescindible. Lo demás no me importa. Quiero que Sebas también me escriba. Quiero saber en que está, trabajo, vida afectiva, etc. etc. Ah ! Y estoy 100% de acuerdo para que no me llames a la madrugada del domingo. Yo sufro mucho pensando en tu trasnoche y las horas de espera, y el cansancio y todo. Yo sigo oyendo el programa por solidaridad con los demás pero descanso sabiendo que tu estás calientita dormida en tu camita.

Bueno, como te decía, la vida aquí no es vida, es un desperdicio lugubre de tiempo. Vivo o sobrevivo en una hamaca tendida entre dos palos, cubierta con un mosquitero y con una carpa encima, que oficia de techo, con lo cual puedo pensar que tengo una casa. Tengo una repisa donde pongo mi equipo, es decir, el morral con la ropa y la Biblia que es mi único lujo. Todo listo para salir corriendo. Aquí nada es propio, nada dura, la incertidumbre y la precariedad son la única constante. En cualquier momento dan la orden de empaquar y duerme uno en cualquier hueco, tendido en cualquier sitio, como cualquier animal. Esos momentos son especialmente difícíles para mí. Me sudan las manos y se me nubla la mente y termino haciendo las cosas dos veces más despacio que lo normal. Las marchas son un calvario porque mi equipo es muy pesado y no puedo con él. A veces los guerilleros llevan cosas mías para aliviarme la carga y me dejan « los tarros », es decir lo de aseo que es lo que más pesa, pero todo eso es estresante, se pierden mis cosas o me las quitan, como el bluyin que Mela ma había regalado en Navidad con el que me cogieron. No lo volví a ver. Lo único que he podido salvar es la chaqueta que ha sido una bendición, porque las noches son heladas y yo no he tenido más que echarme encima para no sentir frío. Antes disfrutaba cada baño en el río. Como soy la única mujer del grupo, me toca prácticamente vestida : shorts, camiseta, botas. Así me baño como las abuelitas nuestras. Antes me gustaba nadar en el río. Hoy ni siquiera tengo alientos para eso. Estoy débil, friolenta, parezco un gato acercándose al agua. Yo que tanto he adorado el agua, ni me reconozco. Durante el día tenía la costumbre de hacer unas dos horas, casi tres, de ejercicios. Ma había inventado un aparatico, como un banquito hecho de palos, que lo bautice « step » pensando en los ejercicios del gimnasio. La idea es subir y bajar como si fuera un escalón : Tiene la ventaja de que no se necesita mucho espacio para hacerlo ; porque hay veces que los campamentos los hacen tan pequeños que queda uno prácticamente encima de otro prisionero. Pero desde que separaron los grupos no he tenido ni el interés, ni la energía para hacer nada. Hago algo de estiramiento porque el estrés me bloquea el cuello y me duele mucho. Con los ejercicios de estiramiento, el split y demás logro aliviar un poco la tensión en el cuello. Eso es todo, Mamita. Yo trato de guardar silencio, hablo lo menos posible para evitar problemas. La presencia de una mujer en medio de tantos prisioneros que llevan 8 o 10 años cautivos es un problema. Oigo en onda corta RFI y la BBC, escribo poquito porque los cuadernos se amontonan y cargar eso es una tortura. Ya he quemado como cuatro. Además, en las requisas le quitan a uno lo que uno más quiere. Una carta que me llegó tuya escrita después de la última prueba de supervivencia en el 2003, los dibujos de Anastasia y Stanis, las fotos de Mela y Loli, el escapulario de mi papá, un programa de gobierno con 190 puntos que había ido anotando durante todos estos años, todo me lo quitaron. Cada día me queda menos de mi misma. Los demás detalles ya Pinchao te los comentó. Todo es duro. Esa es la realidad.

Es importante que le dedique estás lineas a aquellos seres que son mi oxígeno, mi vida. A quienes me mantienen con la cabeza fuera del agua, no me dejan ahogarme en el olvido, la nada y la desesperanza. Ellos son tu, mis hijos, Astrica y mis chiquitines, Fab, tía Nancy y Juanqui.

A mis hijos, los 3, Sebastián, Mela y Loli dales primero mi bendición, para que los acompañe en cada paso que den. Todos los días, estoy en comunicación con Dios, Jesús y la Virgen. A Dios les encomiendo para que nunca les falle su Fe, y para que nunca se aparten de él. Diles que no han cesado de ser mi fuente de alegría en este duro cautiverio. Aqui todo tiene dos caras, la alegría viene con dolor, la felicidad es triste, el amor alivia y abre heridas nuevas, recordar es vivir y morir de nuevo. Durante años no pude pensar en los niños y el dolor de la muerte de mi papá copaba todas mi capacidad de aguante. Cuando pensaba en ellos sentía que me asfixiaba, que no podía respirar. Entonces me decía « Fab está ahí, el cuida de todo, no hay que pensar, no hay que pensar ». Casi me enloquezco con la muerte de mi papá. Necesito hablar con Astrica para hacer mi duelo. Nunca supe cómo fue, quien estaba con él, si me dejo un mensaje, una carta, una bendición. Pero lo que, con los años, ha aliviado mi tormento, es pensar que se fue confiando en Dios y que algun día volveré a abrazarlo. De esto estoy segura. Sentirte fuerte ha sido mi fuerza. . Yo no oí mensajes sino hasta que me unieron con « Lucho » Eladio Pérez, el 22 de agosto del 2003, día del cumpleaños de su hija Carope. Fuimos amigos entrañables, nos separaron en agosto. Pero durante todo ese tiempo él fue mi apoyo, mi escudero, mi hermano. Diles a Angela, a Sergio, a Laura, Marianita y Carope, que los llevo en mi corazón como si fueran de mi familia. Desde esa época he oído tus mensajes con la más increíble constancia, nunca me has fallado. Dios te bendiga. Te decía que durante años no pude pensar en los niños por el dolor horrendo que me producía no estar con ellos. Hoy ya puedo oírlos y sentir más alegría que dolor. Los busco en mis recuerdos y me nutro de las imágenes que guardo en mi memoria de cada uno de sus edades. En cada cumpleaños les canto el « Happy Birthday ». Solicito que me permitan hacer una torta. Antes me colaboraban y yo hacía como algo para marcar la fecha. Pero desde hace tres años, siempre que pido, la respuesta es No. Igual, si traen una galleta o una comida cualquiera de arroz y frijoles, que es lo usual, con eso hago de cuenta que es una torta y les celebro en mi corazón su cumpleaños. Quiero que sepan que el 8 de Abril, el 6 de Sept., el 1ro de Oct. Son sagrados para mi (también celebro el 31 de Dic. El 18 de Julio, el 9 de Agosto, el 1 de Sept, el 24 de Junio y el 31 de Oct, (los últimos son de tía Nancy y Pachao, espero no equivocarme).

A mi Mela, mi sol de primavera, mi princesa de la constelación del cisne, a ella que tanto adoro, quiero decirle que soy la mamá más orgullosa de esta tierra. He tenido tanta suerte, he sido tan bendecida por Dios de tener estos hijos míos, y esta Mela mía que es como el premio gordo de la vida. Tengo, como desde que tenía cinco años y me discutía con inteligencia y bondad, la mayor admiración por mi Mela. Le sobra sabiduría y luz . Y si tuviera que morir hoy me iría satisfecha con la vida, dándole gracias a Dios por mis hijos. Estoy feliz con su Master en NY. Eso es exactamente lo que yo le hubiera aconsejado. El cine es su pasión y estoy 100% con ella en todo. Pero ojo : es muy importante que haga su DOCTORADO. En el mundo de hoy, hasta para respirar se necesitan credenciales. Acceder a un doctorado es estar en otra espera, en otro mundo, de mayor exigencia y disciplina. Y es conocer a los mejores de lo mejor. No me voy a cansar en insistirle a Loli y Mela que no claudiquen hasta obtener su PhD. Quisiera que Mela me prometiera que lo va a hacer, que va a buscar por internet, desde ya aunque esto le pueda parecer todavía remoto y lejano, que va a meterse en las páginas de Harvard, Stanford, Yale, etc. Y va a revisar que doctorados ofrecen, en lo que se le ocurra, lo que más la intrigue, historia, filosofía, arquelogía, teología, que busque y sueñe y se entusiasme, y lo haga su misión personal. Yo sé que ella quiere trabajar, a todos nos pica el reto de empezar a producir, a saber quien somos en realidad, pero esto es algo que debe quedar inscrito en sus planes de vida. A mayor fuerza, mayor alcanze, mayores oportunidades, más grande el universo al que se pueda acceder. Mi Mela, tu sabes que eso es vital, me fascinó que hubieras estudiado filo y no Sces-po, me fascinó que te hayas metido a aprender italiano y ruso, si tengo la oportunidad, si la vida me la da, trataré de alcanzarte ! Soy tu Fan n°1. No tengo palabras para decirte lo que valoro tu trajectoria, la lucidez de tus decisiones, la madurez del camino escogido y de cómo lo recoges. Sé que la academia de cine en que estás es un must y me quito el sombrero. Siempre te he dicho que eres lo mejor, mucho mejor que yo, algo así como la mejor versión de lo que yo quisiera ser. Por eso, con la experiencia que he acumulado en mi vida y con la perspectiva que da del mundo mirarlo desde la distancia, te pido, mi vida, que te prepares para llegar a la cumbre.

A mi Lorenzo, mi Lolipop, mi angel de luz, mi rey de aguas azules, mi chief musician, que me canta y me encanta, al dueño de mi corazón, quiero decirle que desde el día en que nació hasta hoy, ha sido mi manantial de alegrías. Todo lo que viene de él es bálsamo para mi alma, todo me reconforta, todo me apacigua, todo me da placer y placidez. Es mi niño divino, mi pedacito de sol. Cómo quiero verlo, besarlo, abrazarlo y oírlo ! Al fin pude oírle la voz, un par de veces este año ! Me dio temblor de la emoción. Es mi Loli, es la voz de mi niño, pero ya hay otro hombre encima de la voz de niño, una ronquera de hombre hombre, como la de mi papá. ¿ Será que también le heredó las manos a mi papá, esas manotas hermosas que tanto añoro ? ¿ Será que Dios me dió ese doble regalo ? El otro día recorté una foto en la prensa que llegó de casualidad. Es una propaganda de un perfume de Carolina Herrera « 212 Sexy Men », sale un muchacho joven y pensé, así debe estar mi Lorenzo, y la guardé ! Te quiero tanto vida mía, me acuerdo cuando cantaste en el techo del Planetario, siempre supe que tenías alma de artista y voz de Angel. Me siento bendecida por Dios sabiendo que tocas guitarra como un dios ! Te acuerdas de la profesora que iba a la casa a darte clases cuando eras chiquito. Te estoy viendo ! Siempre me intrigaba que la profesora me dijera que eras muy buen alumno cuando yo nunca te oía practicar. Pero sí que me acuerdo de tus ojitos brillantes de felicidad cuando llegaba la profe para la clase o cuando se iba. De eso me acuerdo mucho. Y de tantas otras cosas mi corazón. Tengo tantas ganas de acurruncharme y dormir abrazadita a ti, asi como hacíamos hasta antecitos que me cogieran. Tantas ganas tengo de llenarte de besitos y de oírte, de hablar contigo durante horas para que me cuentes todo, y yo contarte todo. Supe que sacaste 13,75 en el bac. Te cuento que me ganaste. Que orgullosa estoy de ti, mi corazón. Me encanta tu doble diploma de Derecho y Eco en la Sorbonne. Excelente. Me encanta. Pienso que no deberías descartar lo de Sces-po. Son las mismas materias en especial si coges Eco-fi. Pensalo, podrías presentar el examen en Sept del 2008, ya tendrías un año de Sorbonne. Es una escuela prestigiosa, que te abre todas las puertas que quieras. Y tu puedes, eres brillante. Pero eso sí, no descuides tu música, eso lo llevas en los genes. Y como a Mela, a ti también te insisto, Master y luego Ph-D. Tienes la vida por delante. Busquen llegar a lo más alto, estudiar es crecer, no sólo por lo que se aprende intelectualmente, sino por la experiencia humana, la gente alrededor de uno, que lo alimenta a uno emocionalmente pata tener cada día mayor control sobre uno mismo, y espiritualmente, para moldear un carácter de servicio a los demás, donde el ego se reduzca a su más minimal expresión, y se crezca en humildad y fuerza moral. Una va con otra. Eso es vivir, crecer para servir. Por eso tu música es tan importante. Con ella puedes llevar felicidad, compasión, solidaridad, compromiso. Y con tu carrera puedes entender cómo funciona nuestra sociedad, códigos, reglas, y tambén soluciones para lograr un mundo mejor. Les digo a ambos lo mismo, estoy demasiado agradecida de ser la mamá de seres humanos tan especiales y que me deslumbran tanto. Estoy 100% contigo, vida mía. Contigo en todas y para lo que quieras. Sí, soy tu fan n°1, hasta recorto la foto de mi ídolo como una adolescente ! Gracias por darme tanta felicidad.

A mi Sebastián adorado, mi Babou bleu, mi pequeño príncipe de viajes astrales y ancestrales, tanto quiero decirle ! Primero, que no quiero irme de este mundo sin que él tenga el conocimiento, la certeza, y la confirmación, de que no son 2 sino 3 mis hijos del alma, los que Dios me dió y que estan inscritos como tales en el libro de la vida. Lo llevo en mi alma, atravesado todos los días recordándolo como lo ví el primer día con su disfraz del Zorro sobre sus cinco añitos y sus ojitos azules descubriendo un mundo que cambiaba demasiado rápido. Son horas las que quiero hablar con él, como horas con mi Mela y horas con mi Loli. Eso, con él tendré que desenredar años de silencios que me pesan demasiado desde este cautiverio. Decirle que mi color favorito es el azul de sus ojos, con una pizca del morado claro de un pareo que me regaló hace muchos años en las Seychelles. Con ese morado claro me voy a vestir mucho si salgo del verde carcel de esta selva. Y quiero que me enseñe el moonwalk, y tantas otras cosas que quiero aprender de él. Pero sobretodo quiero que sepa que pienso que es muy buen mozo como su mamá, muy inteligente como su papá, y que tiene de mi el mismo carácter, lo cual, algunas veces, puede ser una ventaja. Pero por lo general es un gran Karma. Por eso cada vez que pienso en ti vida mía, me río de ambos, de ti y de mi. Cómo hemos dado de vueltas para terminar exactamente donde empezamos : queriendonos con el alma entera. Sí, mi Babou, tengo que hablar contigo, pedirte perdón por tantos momentos donde no estuve a la altura, pedirte perdón por mi immadurez cuando tenía que protegerte, y cubrirte con mi amor, y darte fuerzas para la vida. Pedirte perdón por no haberme atrevido a buscarte, a ir por ti, a decirte : « Todo puede cambiar menos mi amor por ti ». Por si acaso no llego a salir de aqui, te lo escribo para que lo guardes en tu alma, mi Babou adorado, y para que entiendas lo que yo entendí cuando tus hermanos nacieron y es que siempre te he querido como al hijo que eres y que Dios me dió. Lo demás son formalidades.

Tengo que hablar de mi Fab ahora mismo. Cómo no decirle a él que esos niños nuestros son mi felicidad. Que los momentos más felices de mi vida estan enmarcados por su amor y su presencia, por su ingenio, su vitalidad, son luminosos nuestros hijos. Como nos dijo mi papá a Astrid y a mi, « son esplendorosos » ! ! Y me dirijo a Fab porque a él le debo todo esto, la vida que he llevado enhebrada con el hilo de ese amor incondicional que nunca se ha roto, por ese compromiso eterno de amarnos por encima de todo, que nos juramos en Monguí, y que nunca hemos incumplido. El amor, sólo el amor, puede explicar lo que somos, él y yo, no con las convenciones y rituales del mundo, pero sí con el espíritu del amor de Dios que lo da todo sin condiciones. Yo sé que Fab ha sufrido mucho por mi. Pero que su sufrimiento tenía alivio en saber que él ha sido fuente de paz para mi. Esta prueba que Dios nos mandó es para que crezcamos, para que seamos mejores seres humanos, para que desechemos todo aquello que no sirva y hace bulto en el alma humana. El camino lo estamos recorriendo juntos aunque estemos separados. Y nuestro esfuerzo y nuestra lucha, es luz para nuestros hijos. El es mi mayor consuelo, porque está él ahí, yo sé que mis niños estan bien, y si ellos estan bien, nada de lo demás es grave. Dile a Fab que en él me recuesto, sobre sus hombros lloro, en él me apoyo para seguir sonriendo de tristeza, su amor me hace fuerte. Porque está él al frente de las necesidades de mis hijos, puedo terminar de respirar sin que duela tanto la vida, también sé que si tu Mamita algo necesitaras, Fabrice estaría ahí para ti, como siempre lo ha estado para mi. Sé que Fab está pendiente de donde vive Mela, de donde vive Loli. Entonces me angustio menos. Y estoy tan orgullosa de como ha luchado por mi. Varias veces lo he oído por radio y cómo lo he abrazado en mi corazón a cada palabra cuando se le quiebra la voz y me hace llorar hacia adentro para que nadie lo note. Gracias mi Fab por ser tan divino.

A mi Astrica, tantas cosas que no sé por donde empezar. De pronto decirle que su « hojita de vida » me salvó durante el primer año de secuestro, durante el año de duelo de mi papá. Sé que solo ella puede entender lo que la muerte de papí fue para mi. Mi consuelo siempre será que ella estaba junto a él, y a través de ella, yo también. Necesito tanto hablar con ella de todos estos momentos, y abrazarla y llorar hasta que se me agote el pozo de lágrimas que tengo en el cuerpo. En todo lo que hago durante el día ella está como referencia. Siempre pienso : « Esto lo hacía con Astrid cuando éramos chiquititas », o « Esto lo hacia Astrid mejor que yo » o « Si Astrid estuviera aquí » o « A Dios gracias a Astrid no le tocó ver esto, se hubiera muerto del asco ! » o « del miedo », etc. Cómo entiendo ahora tantas reacciones que ella tenía, cosas que no le gustaban o no soportaba. Cómo la entiendo ahora cuando se irritaba conmigo por mis actitudes o expresiones. Ahora entiendo tantas cosas de mi Astrica y me siento tant cerquitita y tan pegadita a ella. La he oido varias veces por radio. Siento mucha admiración por su impecable expresion, por la calidad de su reflexión, por el dominio de sus emociones, por la elegancia de sus sentimientos. La oigo y pienso « quiero ser así ». Siempre he pensado que es intelectualmente muy superior a mi. Pero he descubierto adicionalmente que con estos años ha brotado en ella una sabiduría que irradia cuando habla. Por todo esto es que me paso el día entero dándole gracias a Dios. Sé lo mucho que le debo a ella y a Daniel. No se imaginan la felicidad cuando me enteré de que se había casado ! Sé que mi papá desde el cielo está feliz, como yo desde esta selva ! Daniel es para mi un ser muy especial, si a mi me hubieran preguntado yo hubiera querido que él fuera el marido de Astrid, el « papá adoptivo » de Anastasia y Stanis, y mi cuñado. Me gusta su inteligencia, su bondad y su prudencia. Esas tres cualidades raramente llegan juntas y cuando se presentan procuran admiración y respeto. Eso siento yo por Daniel, admiración y respeto. Que linda familia, Dios hace bien las cosas. Me imagino como gozan con Anastasia y Stanis. Yo muero de amor por ellos... cómo me ha dolido que me quitaran sus dibujos. El poema de Anastasia decía, « por un golpe de suerte, por un golpe de magia o un golpe de Dios, en tres años o 3 días, estarás de vuelta con nosotros ». Y el dibujo de Stanis era un rescate con helicóptero, yo dormida en una caleta igualita a las de aquí, y él era mi salvador. Adoro a mis dos chiquitines como si fueran mis hijos. Además porque Anastasia es igualita a mi, aunque creo que ya me ganó montando a caballo. Quiero ir a clases con ella a l'Ecole Militaire. Y Stanis porque es mi ahijado y tengo que llevarlo a comer muchos helados a los Campos Eliseos ! Que niños tan divinos. Gózalos Astrid, cada edad es un poema que no vuelve más. Tómales fotos, gravelos en video, ya en DVD me imagino ! Ya estoy anticuada en tecnología. Hágalo para yo poder verlos a sus diferentes edades algun día. Y me acuerdo de Stanis metiendome la punta de la espada plástico de disfraz de mosquetero en el ojo, y mi papá feliz de la vida celebrando la pilatuna. Tesoros en el corazón. Me hacen mucha, mucha, mucha falta.

A Juanqui ¿ Donde estás ? Sólo de vez en cuando lo oigo. Me gusta cuando manda mensajes, siempre me cuenta de los niños y eso, él lo sabe, es felicidad pura para mi. Pero estoy consciente de lo cruel y lo difícil que es esta separación. Entiendo todo y lo sigo queriendo como aquel día en que contabamos las estrellas fugaces tendidos en la playa. Dile que esté en paz con él mismo y conmigo. Que si la vida nos da oportunidad, saldremos fortalecidos de esta prueba.

Quiero decirle a mi tía Nancy que la llevo constantemente en la mente y el corazón. Que lo mejor que ha hecho por mi es estar junto a ti. Que le he rogado a Dios que me de la oportunidad de demostrarle cuanto la quiero, cuanto la siento mía, como otra verdadera mamá que es para mi. Y a través de ella, siempre le mando mis energías de amor a todos, Danilo, Maria Adelaída, Sebas y Tomás, Alix y Michael, Jonathan, Matthew y Andrew, Pacho adorado, Cuquín y la novia. Estoy feliz de que Pacho haya vuelto a Colombia. Como quisiera estar ahí para ayudarlo en el starter. Pedro lo hará sin duda mejor que yo. Y cómo me hubiera gustado estar en esta comida con Toño. Ha sido como volver atrás. Los quiero tanto a todos ! Estoy segura que a Pacho le va a ir muy muy bien. Y siento la buena energía que me manda con el « Nam-myoho-renge-kyo ».

Mamita, son tantas las personas a la cuales quiero darles las gracias por acordarse de nosotros, por no habernos abandonado. Durante mucho tiempo hemos sido como los leprosos que afean el baile, los secuestrados no somos un tema « politicamente correcto », suena mejor decir que hay que ser fuertes frente a la guerilla aún si se sacrifican algunas vidas humanas. Ante eso, el silencio. Sólo el tiempo puede abrir las conciencias y elevar los espíritus. Pienso en la grandeza de los Estados Unidos, por ejemplo. Esa grandeza no es el fruto de la riqueza en tierras, materias primas etc., sino el fruto de la grandeza de alma de los líderes que moldearon la Nación. Cuando Lincoln defendió el derecho a la vida y a la libertad de los esclavos negros de América, también se enfrentó con muchos Floridas y Praderas. Muchos intereses económicos y políticos que consideraban que eran superiores a la vida y a la libertad de un puñado de negros. Pero Lincoln ganó, y quedó impreso en el colectivo de esa nación la prioridad de la vida del ser humano sobre cualquier otro interés. En Colombia tenemos que pensar de dónde venimos, quienes somos y a donde queremos ir. Yo aspiro a que algún día tengamos esa sed de grandeza que hace surgir a los pueblos de la nada hacia el sol. Cuando seamos incondicionales ante la defensa de la vida y de la libertad de los nuestros, es decir, cuando seamos menos individualistas y más solidarios, menos indiferentes y más comprometidos, menos intolerantes y más compasivos, entonces ese día seremos la nación grande que todos quisiéramos que fuéramos. Esta grandeza está ahí dormidita en los corazones. Pero los corazones se han endurecido y pesan tanto que no permiten sentimientos elevados.

Pero hay mucha gente que quisiera agradecer porque están contribuyendo a despertar los espíritus y a engrandecer a Colombia. No puedo mencionarlos a todos pero sí a algunos. Al Presidente Alfonso López y en general a los ex presidentes liberales. Pero al presidente López porque su muerte ha sido especialmente dolorosa para nosotros. También he lamentado no poder volver a abrazar a Hernán Echavarría, de quien tanto aprendí y a quien tanto le debo. Sea este el momento para manifestarle mi admiración y profundo afecto, a las familiad de los diputados, Juan Carlos Narvaez, Alberto Giraldo, Alberto Barraga, Alberto Quintero, Ramiro Echeverry, John Jairo Hoyos, Edison Pérez. A cada uno lo llevo en mis oraciones, y no los olvido ni por un minuto, como un homenaje a la vida que queda en mi y que le pertenece.

Mamita, ya vinieron por las cartas. No voy a alcanzar a escribir todo lo que quisiera. A Piedad y a Chávez, todo mi afecto y mi admiración. Nuestras vidas estan ahí, en el corazón de ellos que sé que es grande y valeroso. Al presidente Chávez, cómo quisiera contarle tantas cosas, y sobre todo cómo disfruto con su manera de ser tan espontánea y generosa cuando lo oigo por la radio en *Aló Presidente*. Me tocó cuando llegaron los niños vallenatos a cantarle. Fue un momento sublime de ternura y hermandad entre colombianos y venezolanos. Gracias por haberse interesado por esta causa, que es la nuestra, y que es tan poco llamativa, porque el dolor ajeno, cuando hace parte de las estadísticas, no le interesa a nadie.

Gracias Presidente.

Gracias también a Alvaro Leyva. Estuvo él cerca, pero las guerras que abogan contra la libertad de este puñado de olvidados son como un hurracán que todo lo quiere derribar. No interesa. Su inteligencia, su nobleza, y su constancia, han hecho reflexionar a muchos, y aquí, más que la libertad de unos pobres locos encadenados en la selva, se trata de tomar conciencia de lo que significa defender la dignidad del ser humano. Gracias Alvaro.

Gracias a Lucho Garzón, por su compromiso, su compasión, su generosidad y su constancia. Aquí también las luciérnagas encendieron la selva a la hora del concierto. Aquí también cantamos con la voz de la esperanza.

Gracias a Gustavo Petro por recordarnos con fotos en el recinto, y en sus discursos, y cada vez que puede. Y lo mismo a tantos amigos que nos ayudan con sus comentarios de apoyo y de ánimo, desde el Polo, desde el Partido liberal. Gracias a todos por no dejarnos en el olvido, por no resignarse al olvido de los secuestrados.

He oído a Juan Gabriel Uribe varias veces aportando sus luces y sus conocimientos para favorecer la posibilidad de una liberación. Lo mismo a Sahiel Hernández y a Claudia López. Gracias.

Gracias y felicitaciones a los premiados con el Galardón Bolívar, quienes no han dejado de abandonar la causa de la libertad. En especial a Julio Sánchez Cristo. Mil veces gracias por el compromiso y la ternura. A Daniel Coronel por la valentía y la constancia, y de nuevo a Juan Gabriel Uribe por la reflexión constructiva y la inmensa compasión por nosotros.

Y es que nosotros le debemos demasiado a los medios. Es por ellos que no nos hemos vuelto del todo locos en la sola soledad de la selva. A Erwin Hoyos, felicitaciones por su premio y mis agradecimientos constantes y cumulativos por su programa *Las Voces del Secuestro*, cuyas miles de horas transmitiendo mensajes de nuestras familias equivalen a miles de horas de receso de la angustia y la desesperanza. Dios lo bendiga.

Lo mismo a Nelson Moreno, Fernando Obando, Manuel Fernando Ochoa y todos los miembros de la *Carrilera de las 5*. Hemos vivido sacando ánimos para abrir los ojos durante estos interminables años, y gracias a la música de inicio del programa que actúa como feliz augurio del único contacto que nos ha quedado con nuestras familias. Dios nos de la posibilidad de algún día ir a abrazarlos para devolverles algo de la buena energía con la que llenan sus voces y nuestros corazones, cada día de cada mes de cada año de este terrible cautiverio.

También quiero decirle a Dario Arizmendi que todos aquí somos concientes y agradecemos su empeño en mantener nuestro recuerdo vivo. Gracias por mantener la mano tendida. Su voz es la única verdadera fuerza para salir vivos de aquí, porque es la voz que reclama y pide cuentas. Gracias, gracias !

A Juan Gassain, cuantas veces hemos sentido que el sufrimiento nuestro, él lo entiende, y lo hace suyo, y lo siente, y lo transmite, haciendo que esta prueba que nos tocó vivir quede aliviada con la compañia de millones de colombianos que entonces entienden y también comparten nuestros sentimientos de frustración y desesperanza. En los amigos de Todelar, en L. Guillermo Troya y todo su equipo, hemos encontrado interés y compromiso en momentos de abandono y soledad. Siempre han estado ahí para nosotros. Gracias.

Quisiera nombrarlos a todos, pero se me acabó el tiempo. Saludos a J.G. Rios y a tantos más que nos han acompañado todos estos años.

No quiero despedirme sin mandarle un fraternal abrazo a Monseñor Castro, lo mismo que al padre Echeverry. Siempre han estado dando la batalla por nosotros. Siempre han hablado cuando el silencio y el olvido nos tapan más que la selva misma. Dios los ilumine y los guie para que pronto podamos hablar de todo esto al pasado. Y si no, si Dios tiene otros planes, nos veremos, no lo dudo, en el mismo cielo, dándole gracias a Dios por su infinita misericordia.

Mi corazón también le pertenece a Francia. Y el « también » sobra. « Mon cœur appartient à la France, ma douce France qui m'a tant donné ». Escribo en español para no crear suspicacias que dificulten el tránsito de esta carta. Cuando pienso en Dios, y pienso en su bendición sobre todos nosotros, pienso en Francia. La providencia busca expresarse a través de canales de sabiduría y de amor. Desde el inicio de este secuestro Francia ha tenido la voz de la sabiduría y del amor. Nunca se ha dado por vencida, nunca ha aceptado el paso del tiempo como única solución, nunca ha claudicado en la defensa de nuestro derecho a ser defendidos. Cuando la noche era la más oscura, Francia fue el faro. Cuando era mal visto pedir por nuestra libertad, Francia no se calló. Cuando acusaron a nuestras familias de hacerle daño a Colombia, Francia les dió apoyo y consuelo. No podría creer que es posible salir algún día libre de aqui, si no conociera la historia de Francia y de su pueblo. Le he pedido a Dios que me nutra de la misma fuerza con la que Francia a sabido soportar la adversidad, para sentirme más digna de ser contada entre sus hijos. Quiero a Francia con el alma, las raíces de mi ser buscan sumirse con los componentes de su carácter nacional, siempre buscando guiarse por principios y no por intereses. Quiero a Francia con mi corazón, porque admiro la capacidad de mobilización de un pueblo que, como Camus, entiende que vivir es comprometerse. Hoy Francia se ha comprometido con los secuestrados de Colombia, como también lo ha hecho con Aung San Suu Kyi ou Ana Politkovskaïa. Siempre en busqueda de la Justicia, de la Libertad, de la Verdad. Quiero a Francia con mi reflexion, porque hay en Francia la elegancia de la constancia para que no parezca terquedad, y la generosidad del compromiso para que no caiga en la obsesión. Mi amor incondicional y eterno a Francia y al pueblo francés es la mayor expresión de mi gratitud. No soy digna ni merezco el cariño que me han brindado y me siento muy poca cosa para siquiera aspirar a respaldo de tantos corazones. Sólo me tranquilizo pensando que el compromiso de Francia es el compromiso con otro pueblo que sufre, es el derecho a auxiliar a otros seres humanos ante el dolor y la muerte, es la decisión de actuar frente a lo inaceptable. Porque definitivamente, todo lo que ha sucedido es simplemente inaceptable. Todo lo que ha sucedido aqui es inaceptable.

El presidente Chirac nos acompañó durante muchos años, siempre firme, siempre claro, siempre compasivo. A él y a Dominique de Villepin, los llevo en mi corazón. Todos estos años han sido terribles, pero no creo que podria seguir aún viva sin el compromiso que nos brindaron a todos los que aqui vivimos muertos. El Presidente Sarkozy ha tomado el liderazgo de profundos cambios en Francia. Estoy convencida que la fuerza de sus convicciones y la nobleza de sus sentimientos abrirán corazones y mentes. Sé que lo que estamos viviendo está lleno de incognitas, pero la historia tiene sus propios tiempos de maduración y el Presidente Sarkozy esta parado sobre el meridiano de la historia. Con el Presidente Chávez y el Presidente Bush y la solidaridad de toto el continente, podriamos presenciar un milagro.

Durante muchos años he pensado que mientras este viva, mientras siga respirando, tengo que seguir albergando la esperanza. Ya no tengo las mismas fuerzas, ya me cuesta mucho trabajo seguir creyendo, pero quiero que sientan que lo que han hecho por nosotros ha hecho la diferencia. Nos hemos sentido seres humanos.

Mamita, tendria más cosas que decirte. Explicarte que hace tiempos no tengo noticias de Clara y de su bebe. Dile a Pinchao que te de detalles, él te contará todo. Es importante que evalues lo que te comente y tengas la posibilidad de poner distancias, tener mucha prudencia.

Sé que has tenido contacto con la mamá de Marc González. El es una persona demasiado especial, de una gran calidad humana. Dile que le mande mensajes por la *Carrilera*, ellos oyen el programa. Yo creo que todos lo hacemos. Ya estoy con otro grupo, pero quiero mucho a Marc, para que le cuentes a Jo que su hijo está bien.

Bueno, no quisiera despedirme. Dios quiera que te llegue esto. Te llevo en el alma mi Mamita linda. Una última recomendación : cualquier cosa económica, que la maneje Astrid (estilo premios, o cosas así). También he pensado que si mi apto está vacío y si no se pagan las cuotas, porque no te vas tú para allá ? Por lo menos eso sería una preocupación menos. Si algo me quieres comentar por radio que sea personal, dímelo en francés para que yo capte de que me vas a hablar, y sigues en español. Podríamos hablar del « tio Jorge » por ejemplo, y yo entendería. Bueno, Mamita, Dios nos ayude, nos guie, nos de paciencia y nos cubra.

Por siempre y para siempre, tu hija,

Ingrid Betancourt, 15:34

Text copyright © 2008 by Ingrid Betancourt, Melanie Delloye-Betancourt,
and Lorenzo Delloye-Betancourt
English translation copyright © 2008 by Krister Swartz and Miranda Ottewell
French translation copyright © 2008 by Le Seuil
Elie Wiesel's foreword copyright © 2008 by Elirion Associates

Published in 2008 by Abrams Image
An imprint of Harry N. Abrams, Inc.

Library of Congress Cataloging-in-Publication Data
Betancourt, Ingrid, 1961-
  Letters to my mother : a message of love, a plea for freedom / by Ingrid Betancourt,
Lorenzo Delloye-Betancourt & Melanie Delloye-Betancourt ; foreword by Elie Wiesel ;
introduction by Dominique Simonnet.
    p. cm.
  ISBN 978-0-8109-7127-1
  1. Betancourt, Ingrid, 1961–Correspondence. 2. Betancourt, Ingrid, 1961–Kidnapping,
2002-3. Pulecio Betancourt, Yolanda–Correspondence. 4. Delloye-Betancourt,
Lorenzo–Correspondence. 5. Delloye-Betancourt, Mélanie–Correspondence. 6. Kidnapping victims–Colombia–Correspondence. I. Delloye-Betancourt, Lorenzo. II. Delloye-
Betancourt, Mélanie. III. Title.
  F2279.22.B48A4 2008
  986.106'35–dc22
  2008004006

Editors: Ann Stratton and Dominique Simonnet
Designers: Liam Flanagan and Galen Smith
Production Manager: Jacqueline Poirier

The text of this book was composed in Bodoni Twelve ITC.

Printed and bound in the U.S.A.
10 9 8 7 6 5 4 3 2 1

HNA ■■■■■
harry n. abrams, inc.
a subsidiary of La Martinière Groupe

115 West 18th Street
New York, NY 10011
www.hnabooks.com